Library and Archives Canada Cataloguing in Publication available upon request.

ISBN 978-0-7710-5737-3

Published simultaneously in the United States of America by
Fenn/McClelland & Stewart, a division of Random House of Canada Limited,
a Penguin Random House Company

Library of Congress Control Number: 2013931568

Printed and bound in the United States of America

McClelland & Stewart,
a division of Random House of Canada Limited,
a Penguin Random House Company
One Toronto Street
Toronto, Ontario
M5C 2V6
www.randomhouse.ca

1   2   3   4   5   17   16   15   14   13

FENN
M & S

CONTENTS

6   Introduction

16   How the Red Sox Were Built

17   Regular-Season Results

19   Regular-Season Stats

20   American League Division Series Recap

32   American League Championship Series Recap

52   World Series Recap

79   2013 Postseason Stats

82   Postseason History

88   Inside the World Series

98   Fenway Park

100   Birth of the Red Sox

101   2013 Boston Red Sox Roster

132   2013: Season in Review

148 B Strong
In the wake of an early-season tragedy, the Red Sox became a unifying force for the city of Boston.

150 Mane Attractions
A wild array of beards put a quirky new face on the game this season, and the Sox were the hairiest of the bunch.

154 The Toast of Beantown
From triumphs to struggles and back again, Dustin Pedroia has endured it all during his tenure in Boston. This year's return to glory and a new contract extension promise to keep the bond between the city and its second baseman tight.

159 Minor League Results

160 Acknowledgments

ON MARCH 30, 2013, 43 baseball experts at ESPN submitted their yearly predictions for the MLB season. Just four of them picked the Red Sox to make the postseason. None of them had Boston winning the AL pennant, and of course, the World Series was an afterthought. But it's not fair to vilify pundits who believed a 69-win team from a year ago couldn't contend for a title, because not even the most prescient among us could have predicted what would happen next.

From early-season tragedy rose spectacular triumph, as the rag-tag bearded bunch put a grief-stricken city on its back and rode a wave of unbridled support and emotion to a dream season. An incredible 97 wins and an AL pennant later, the Red Sox were poised to wash away sour memories of the worst season in recent franchise history and restore glory to Boston. But it would not come easy against a St. Louis Cardinals juggernaut with a stacked lineup and a prodigious pitching staff.

Much like it was from April to September, the Red Sox's October crusade was a consummate team effort, in which contributions came from big and small, first-year Sox and 10-year veterans, powerhouse hitters and savvy scrappers. Leading the charge on offense, to no one's surprise, was David Ortiz. Big Papi took home Series MVP honors with an otherworldly effort, securing the highest career Fall Classic batting average ever for hitters with at least 50 plate appearances and cementing his status as a postseason legend. Not far behind were Red Sox lifers Dustin Pedroia and Jacoby Ellsbury, who seemed to be making key plays at every turn. Slugging newcomers Mike Napoli and Jonny Gomes hit their share of dramatic longballs, and seasoned playoff veteran Shane Victorino knocked the two most important shots of the season: a grand slam that sealed the AL pennant and a three-run double in the clinching game of the World Series. Staff ace Jon Lester and crafty veteran John Lackey rose to the occasion, while closer Koji Uehara prolonged his torrid regular-season stretch, finishing October with seven saves and a 0.66 ERA.

When it was all said and done, first-year manager John Farrell's squad had completed the biggest statistical turnaround ever: No team had ever won a World Series coming off a year with a winning percentage as low as Boston's .426 in 2012. "The one thing that really stood out more than anything was their overall will to win," said Farrell. "And that was no more evident than in this entire postseason."

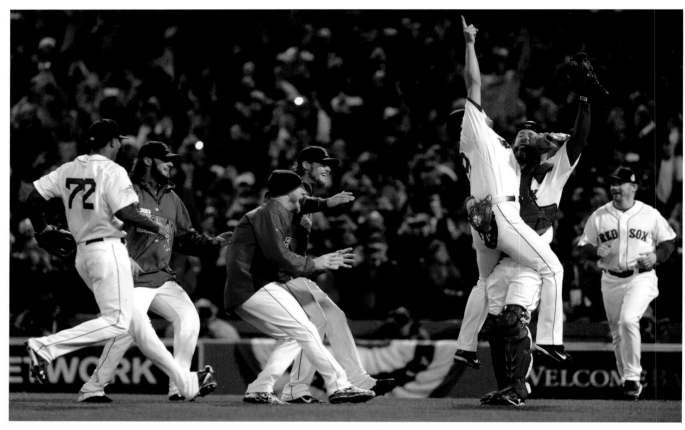

ASSEMBLING THE PIECES

REBUILDING A TEAM from cellar dweller to World Series champion in just one offseason is no easy feat. The coalescence of the 2013 Red Sox was thus an unorthodox, unprecedented union. Red Sox lifers drafted years back were joined by trade acquisitions and a melting pot of free-agent signings — some new for this season, some nabbed a bit further back, and one inked a decade ago. But on a team where chemistry flowed as abundantly as facial hair, tenure never seemed to matter.

TRADE

Andrew Bailey	From OAK with Ryan Sweeney for Miles Head, Raul Alcantara and Josh Reddick (2011)
Quintin Berry	From KC for Clayton Mortensen (2013)
Craig Breslow	From ARI for Matt Albers and Scott Podsednik (2012)
Mike Carp	From SEA for player to be named later or cash (2013)
Joel Hanrahan	From PIT with Brock Holt for Ivan De Jesus, Mark Melancon, Stolmy Pimentel and Jerry Sands (2012)
Brock Holt	From PIT with Joel Hanrahan for Ivan De Jesus, Mark Melancon, Stolmy Pimentel and Jerry Sands (2012)
Franklin Morales	From COL for cash (2011)
Daniel Nava	Purchased from Chico (Golden League, 2008)
Jake Peavy	From CHW with Brayan Villarreal (from DET) for Cleuluis Rondon, Francellis Montas, Jeffrey Wendelken (to CHW) and Jose Iglesias (to DET)
Jarrod Saltalamacchia	From TEX for Roman Mendez, Chris McGuiness, Michael Thomas and cash (2010)
Allen Webster	From LAD with Ivan De Jesus, James Loney, Rubby De La Rosa and Jerry Sands for Josh Beckett, Carl Crawford, Adrian Gonzalez, Nick Punto and cash (2012)

DRAFT

Jackie Bradley Jr.	1st round, 2011
Drake Britton	23rd round, 2007
Clay Buchholz	1st round, 2005
Jacoby Ellsbury	1st round, 2005
Ryan Lavarnway	6th round, 2008
Jon Lester	2nd round, 2002
Will Middlebrooks	5th round, 2007
Dustin Pedroia	2nd round, 2004
Alex Wilson	2nd round, 2009
Brandon Workman	2nd round, 2010

FREE AGENCY

Xander Bogaerts	Pre-arbitration eligible (2009)
Ryan Dempster	2 years/$26.5M (2013)
Felix Doubront	Pre-arbitration eligible (2005)
Stephen Drew	1 year/$9.5M (2012)
Jonny Gomes	2 years/$10M (2012)
John Lackey	5 years/$82.5M, 2015 vesting option (2009)
Andrew Miller	1 year/$1.48M, second-year arbitration eligible (2010)
Mike Napoli	1 year/$13M (2013)
David Ortiz	2 years/$26M (2012)
David Ross	2 years/$6.2M (2012)
Junichi Tazawa	Pre-arbitration eligible (2008)
Koji Uehara	2 years/$9.25M (2012)
Shane Victorino	3 years/$39M (2012)

REGULAR-SEASON RESULTS

DATE	OPP.	RES.	R	RA	W-L
Monday, April 1	@ NYY	W	8	2	1-0
Wednesday, April 3	@ NYY	W	7	4	2-0
Thursday, April 4	@ NYY	L	2	4	2-1
Friday, April 5	@ TOR	W	6	4	3-1
Saturday, April 6	@ TOR	L	0	5	3-2
Sunday, April 7	@ TOR	W	13	0	4-2
Monday, April 8	BAL	W	3	1	5-2
Wednesday, April 10	BAL	L	5	8	5-3
Thursday, April 11	BAL	L	2	3	5-4
Saturday, April 13	TB	W	2	1	6-4
Sunday, April 14	TB	W	5	0	7-4
Monday, April 15	TB	W	3	2	8-4
Tuesday, April 16	@ CLE	W	7	2	9-4
Wednesday, April 17	@ CLE	W	6	3	10-4
Thursday, April 18	@ CLE	W	6	3	11-4
Saturday, April 20	KC	W	4	3	12-4
Sunday, April 21 (1)	KC	L	2	4	12-5
Sunday, April 21 (2)	KC	L	4	5	12-6
Monday, April 22	OAK	W	9	6	13-6
Tuesday, April 23	OAK	L	0	13	13-7
Wednesday, April 24	OAK	W	6	5	14-7
Thursday, April 25	HOU	W	7	2	15-7
Friday, April 26	HOU	W	7	3	16-7
Saturday, April 27	HOU	W	8	4	17-7
Sunday, April 28	HOU	W	6	1	18-7
Tuesday, April 30	@ TOR	L	7	9	18-8
Wednesday, May 1	@ TOR	W	10	1	19-8
Thursday, May 2	@ TOR	W	3	1	20-8
Friday, May 3	@ TEX	L	0	7	20-9
Saturday, May 4	@ TEX	L	1	5	20-10
Sunday, May 5	@ TEX	L	3	4	20-11
Monday, May 6	MIN	W	6	5	21-11
Tuesday, May 7	MIN	L	1	6	21-12
Wednesday, May 8	MIN	L	8	15	21-13
Thursday, May 9	MIN	L	3	5	21-14
Friday, May 10	TOR	W	5	0	22-14
Saturday, May 11	TOR	L	2	3	22-15
Sunday, May 12	TOR	L	4	12	22-16
Tuesday, May 14	@ TB	L	3	5	22-17
Wednesday, May 15	@ TB	W	9	2	23-17
Thursday, May 16	@ TB	W	4	3	24-17
Friday, May 17	@ MIN	W	3	2	25-17
Saturday, May 18	@ MIN	W	12	5	26-17
Sunday, May 19	@ MIN	W	5	1	27-17
Monday, May 20	@ CHW	L	4	6	27-18
Tuesday, May 21	@ CHW	L	1	3	27-19
Wednesday, May 22	@ CHW	W	6	2	28-19
Thursday, May 23	CLE	L	3	12	28-20
Friday, May 24	CLE	W	8	1	29-20
Saturday, May 25	CLE	W	7	4	30-20
Sunday, May 26	CLE	W	6	5	31-20
Monday, May 27	PHI	W	9	3	32-20
Tuesday, May 28	PHI	L	1	3	32-21
Wednesday, May 29	@ PHI	L	3	4	32-22
Thursday, May 30	@ PHI	W	9	2	33-22
Friday, May 31	@ NYY	L	1	4	33-23
Saturday, June 1	@ NYY	W	11	1	34-23
Sunday, June 2	@ NYY	W	3	0	35-23
Tuesday, June 4	TEX	W	17	5	36-23
Wednesday, June 5	TEX	L	2	3	36-24
Thursday, June 6	TEX	W	6	3	37-24
Saturday, June 8 (1)	LAA	L	5	9	37-25
Saturday, June 8 (2)	LAA	W	7	2	38-25
Sunday, June 9	LAA	W	10	5	39-25
Monday, June 10	@ TB	W	10	8	40-25
Tuesday, June 11	@ TB	L	3	8	40-26
Wednesday, June 12	@ TB	W	2	1	41-26
Thursday, June 13	@ BAL	L	4	5	41-27
Friday, June 14	@ BAL	L	0	2	41-28
Saturday, June 15	@ BAL	W	5	4	42-28
Sunday, June 16	@ BAL	L	3	6	42-29
Tuesday, June 18 (1)	TB	W	5	1	43-29
Tuesday, June 18 (2)	TB	W	3	1	44-29
Wednesday, June 19	TB	L	2	6	44-30
Thursday, June 20	@ DET	L	3	4	44-31
Friday, June 21	@ DET	W	10	6	45-31
Saturday, June 22	@ DET	L	3	10	45-32
Sunday, June 23	@ DET	L	5	7	45-33
Tuesday, June 25	COL	W	11	4	46-33
Wednesday, June 26	COL	W	5	3	47-33
Thursday, June 27	TOR	W	7	4	48-33
Friday, June 28	TOR	W	7	5	49-33
Saturday, June 29	TOR	L	2	6	49-34
Sunday, June 30	TOR	W	5	4	50-34

REGULAR-SEASON RESULTS

DATE	OPP.	RES.	R	RA	W-L
Tuesday, July 2	SD	W	4	1	51-34
Wednesday, July 3	SD	W	2	1	52-34
Thursday, July 4	SD	W	8	2	53-34
Friday, July 5	@ LAA	W	6	2	54-34
Saturday, July 6	@ LAA	L	7	9	54-35
Sunday, July 7	@ LAA	L	0	3	54-36
Monday, July 8	@ SEA	L	4	11	54-37
Tuesday, July 9	@ SEA	W	11	8	55-37
Wednesday, July 10	@ SEA	W	11	4	56-37
Thursday, July 11	@ SEA	W	8	7	57-37
Friday, July 12	@ OAK	W	4	2	58-37
Saturday, July 13	@ OAK	L	0	3	58-38
Sunday, July 14	@ OAK	L	2	3	58-39
Friday, July 19	NYY	W	4	2	59-39
Saturday, July 20	NYY	W	2	5	59-40
Sunday, July 21	NYY	W	8	7	60-40
Monday, July 22	TB	L	0	3	60-41
Tuesday, July 23	TB	W	6	2	61-41
Wednesday, July 24	TB	L	1	5	61-42
Friday, July 26	@ BAL	L	0	6	61-43
Saturday, July 27	@ BAL	W	7	3	62-43
Sunday, July 28	@ BAL	W	5	0	63-43
Monday, July 29	TB	L	1	2	63-44
Tuesday, July 30	SEA	W	8	2	64-44
Wednesday, July 31	SEA	W	5	4	65-44
Thursday, Aug. 1	SEA	W	8	7	66-44
Friday, Aug. 2	ARI	L	6	7	66-45
Saturday, Aug. 3	ARI	W	5	2	67-45
Sunday, Aug. 4	ARI	W	4	0	68-45
Monday, Aug. 5	@ HOU	L	0	2	68-46
Tuesday, Aug. 6	@ HOU	W	15	10	69-46
Wednesday, Aug. 7	@ HOU	W	7	5	70-46
Thursday, Aug. 8	@ KC	L	1	5	70-47
Friday, Aug. 9	@ KC	L	6	9	70-48
Saturday, Aug. 10	@ KC	W	5	3	71-48
Sunday, Aug. 11	@ KC	L	3	4	71-49
Tuesday, Aug. 13	@ TOR	W	4	2	72-49
Wednesday, Aug. 14	@ TOR	L	3	4	72-50
Thursday, Aug. 15	@ TOR	L	1	2	72-51
Friday, Aug. 16	NYY	L	3	10	72-52
Saturday, Aug. 17	NYY	W	6	1	73-52
Sunday, Aug. 18	NYY	L	6	9	73-53
Monday, Aug. 19	@ SF	W	7	0	74-53
Tuesday, Aug. 20	@ SF	L	2	3	74-54
Wednesday, Aug. 21	@ SF	W	12	1	75-54
Friday, Aug. 23	@ LAD	L	0	2	75-55
Saturday, Aug. 24	@ LAD	W	4	2	76-55
Sunday, Aug. 25	@ LAD	W	8	1	77-55
Tuesday, Aug. 27	BAL	W	13	2	78-55
Wednesday, Aug. 28	BAL	W	4	3	79-55
Thursday, Aug. 29	BAL	L	2	3	79-56
Friday, Aug. 30	CHW	W	4	3	80-56
Saturday, Aug. 31	CHW	W	7	2	81-56
Sunday, Sept. 1	CHW	W	7	6	82-56
Monday, Sept. 2	DET	L	0	3	82-57
Tuesday, Sept. 3	DET	W	2	1	83-57
Wednesday, Sept. 4	DET	W	20	4	84-57
Thursday, Sept. 5	@ NYY	W	9	8	85-57
Friday, Sept. 6	@ NYY	W	12	8	86-57
Saturday, Sept. 7	@ NYY	W	13	9	87-57
Sunday, Sept. 8	@ NYY	L	3	4	87-58
Tuesday, Sept. 10	@ TB	W	2	0	88-58
Wednesday, Sept. 11	@ TB	W	7	3	89-58
Thursday, Sept. 12	@ TB	L	3	4	89-59
Friday, Sept. 13	NYY	W	8	4	90-59
Saturday, Sept. 14	NYY	W	5	1	91-59
Sunday, Sept. 15	NYY	W	9	2	92-59
Tuesday, Sept. 17	BAL	L	2	3	92-60
Wednesday, Sept. 18	BAL	L	3	5	92-61
Thursday, Sept. 19	BAL	W	3	1	93-61
Friday, Sept. 20	TOR	W	6	3	94-61
Saturday, Sept. 21	TOR	L	2	4	94-62
Sunday, Sept. 22	TOR	W	5	2	95-62
Tuesday, Sept. 24	@ COL	L	3	8	95-63
Wednesday, Sept. 25	@ COL	W	15	5	96-63
Friday, Sept. 27	@ BAL	W	12	3	97-63
Saturday, Sept. 28	@ BAL	L	5	6	97-64
Sunday, Sept. 29	@ BAL	L	6	7	97-65

REGULAR-SEASON STATS

NO.	PLAYER	B/T	W	L	ERA	SO	BB	SV	BIRTHDATE	BIRTHPLACE
PITCHERS										
32	Craig Breslow	L/L	5	2	1.81	33	18	0	8/8/80	New Haven, CT
11	Clay Buchholz	L/R	12	1	1.74	96	36	0	8/14/84	Nederland, TX
46	Ryan Dempster	R/R	8	9	4.57	157	79	0	5/3/77	Sechelt, Canada
22	Felix Doubront	L/L	11	6	4.32	139	71	0	10/23/87	Carabobo, Venezuela
41	John Lackey	R/R	10	13	3.52	161	40	0	10/23/78	Abilene, TX
31	Jon Lester	L/L	15	8	3.75	177	67	0	1/7/84	Tacoma, WA
56	Franklin Morales	L/L	2	2	4.62	21	15	0	1/24/86	San Juan de los Morros, Venez.
44	Jake Peavy	R/R	12	5	4.17	121	36	0	5/31/81	Mobile, AL
36	Junichi Tazawa	R/R	5	4	3.16	72	12	0	6/6/86	Yokohama, Japan
19	Koji Uehara	R/R	4	1	1.09	101	9	21	4/3/75	Neyagawa, Japan
67	Brandon Workman	R/R	6	3	4.97	47	15	0	8/13/88	Bowie, TX

NO.	PLAYER	B/T	AB	H	AVG	HR	RBI	OBP	BIRTHDATE	BIRTHPLACE
CATCHERS										
3	David Ross	R/R	102	22	.216	4	10	.298	3/19/77	Bainbridge, GA
39	Jarrod Saltalamacchia	S/R	425	116	.273	14	65	.338	5/2/85	West Palm Beach, FL
INFIELDERS										
72	Xander Bogaerts	R/R	44	11	.250	1	5	.320	10/1/92	Oranjestad, Aruba
7	Stephen Drew	L/R	442	112	.253	13	67	.333	3/16/83	Hahira, GA
16	Will Middlebrooks	R/R	348	79	.227	17	49	.271	9/9/88	Greenville, TX
12	Mike Napoli	R/R	498	129	.259	23	92	.360	10/31/81	Hollywood, FL
34	David Ortiz	L/L	518	160	.309	30	103	.395	11/18/75	Santo Domingo, D.R.
15	Dustin Pedroia	R/R	641	193	.301	9	84	.372	8/17/83	Woodland, CA
OUTFIELDERS										
50	Quintin Berry	L/L	8	5	.625	1	4	.667	11/21/84	San Diego, CA
37	Mike Carp	L/R	216	64	.296	9	43	.362	6/30/86	Long Beach, CA
2	Jacoby Ellsbury	L/L	577	172	.298	9	53	.355	9/11/83	Madras, OR
5	Jonny Gomes	R/R	312	77	.247	13	52	.344	11/22/80	Petaluma, CA
29	Daniel Nava	S/L	458	139	.303	12	66	.385	2/22/83	Redwood City, CA
18	Shane Victorino	S/R	477	140	.294	15	61	.351	11/30/80	Wailuku, HI

Manager: John Farrell (53). Coaches: Arnie Beyeler (43), Brian Butterfield (13), Greg Colbrunn (28), Dana LeVangie (58), Torey Lovullo (17), Juan Nieves (47).

GAME 1, OCT. 4
RED SOX 12, RAYS 2

ON THE HEELS OF WINS IN TWO DO-OR-DIE GAMES, Tampa Bay dampened the atmosphere in Boston for a bit as Fenway Park hosted its first postseason game since 2009. Sean Rodriguez and Ben Zobrist connected on home runs in the second and fourth, respectively, but the visitors' lead would soon evaporate.

Thanks in part to a rally-enabling misplay by rookie outfielder Wil Myers, which allowed a David Ortiz ground-rule double to drop in, Boston erupted for five runs in the bottom of the fourth. The offensive onslaught continued with three more in the fifth and four in the eighth, backing 7.2 strong innings of three-hit ball from Jon Lester.

The entire Red Sox lineup recorded a hit in Game 1. Jarrod Saltalamacchia led the way with three RBI, while Shane Victorino and Jonny Gomes each drove in two. It was the first time in 12 years that a team scored at least 12 runs in a postseason game without going yard.

	1	2	3	4	5	6	7	8	9	R	H	E
TAMPA BAY	0	1	0	1	0	0	0	0	0	2	4	0
BOSTON	0	0	0	5	3	0	0	4	x	12	14	0

WP: Lester LP: Moore
HR: TB: Rodriguez, Zobrist

Gomes scored one of the Red Sox's five fourth-inning runs after kick-starting the inning with a two-run double.

Lester went up against the Rays' Matt Moore and easily came out on top thanks to a 12-run offensive explosion. He struck out seven in 7.2 innings.

"WE WERE FORTUNATE TO CATCH A BREAK ON DAVID'S DOUBLE IN THAT FOURTH INNING, AND WE WERE ABLE TO BUNCH SOME HITS AFTER THAT. AND THEN A QUIRKY CAROM OFF THE WALL ON MIDDLEBROOKS'S DOUBLE, AND WE'RE ABLE TO PUT TOGETHER A BIG INNING." John Farrell

GAME 1, OCT. 4
RED SOX 12, RAYS 2

Saltalamacchia went 2 for 4 with three RBI and a run scored, leading a well-balanced, powerful Red Sox attack in Game 1.

"THERE'S NOTHING LIKE PLAYOFF ATMOSPHERE. YOU JUST CAN'T DUPLICATE IT. IT'S A DIFFERENT BEAST WHEN YOU STEP OUT ON THAT MOUND." Jon Lester

Will Middlebrooks knocked a two-out, RBI double in Boston's fourth-inning outburst. He later came around to score on a Victorino single.

GAME 2, OCT. 5
RED SOX 7, RAYS 4

FACING LEFTY ACE DAVID PRICE, THE RED SOX RELIED on the three offensive holdovers from their 2007 World Series team — David Ortiz, Dustin Pedroia and Jacoby Ellsbury — to take care of business in Game 2. On an afternoon in which Boston's starting pitching was shaky — John Lackey allowed seven hits and four earned runs in 5.1 innings — the Sox got their biggest contributions from Ortiz, who hit two solo homers. But small-ball help came from Ellsbury, who went 3 for 4 with a steal and three runs scored, and Pedroia, who had a hit and three RBI.

It wasn't a runaway for Boston, though, as Rays first baseman James Loney cut the home team's four-run lead in half with a two-run double in the fifth. But the Boston bullpen was nearly perfect, with Craig Breslow, Junichi Tazawa and closer Koji Uehara combining for 3.2 innings of one-hit, shutout relief, sealing the 7-4 victory and a 2-games-to-none series lead.

	1	2	3	4	5	6	7	8	9	R	H	E
TAMPA BAY	0	1	0	0	2	1	0	0	0	4	8	2
BOSTON	2	0	2	1	1	0	0	1	x	7	11	0

WP: Lackey LP: Price SV: Uehara
HR: BOS: Ortiz (2)

Ortiz, a centerpiece on both the 2004 and '07 championship squads, proved that his bat was still a force, going deep twice to put the Sox ahead.

Ortiz hoisted Uehara after he notched his first career postseason save.

"IT'S NOT OVER. WE'VE GOT TO KEEP ON FIGHTING. WE KNOW WE'RE PLAYING AGAINST A GOOD BALLCLUB. THEY ALWAYS FIND A WAY TO WIN GAMES, AND YOU CAN'T TAKE ANYTHING FOR GRANTED."
David Ortiz

GAME 3, OCT. 7
RAYS 5, RED SOX 4

THE JOE MADDON–HELMED RAYS ARE AS SYNONYMOUS with resiliency as any team in baseball. So despite being down, 2-0, and going up against Clay Buchholz in their fourth elimination game in nine days, the Rays had no reason to panic upon their return to the Trop.

Although starter Alex Cobb was tagged for a run in the first and two more in the fifth, Evan Longoria gave himself a 28th birthday gift with two on and two out in the bottom of the frame, sending a three-run homer to left to even the score. Tampa took the lead on an RBI groundout by Delmon Young in the bottom of the eighth, but closer Fernando Rodney couldn't hold it, as Boston scratched across a run of its own in the ninth.

Extra innings seemed inevitable after Koji Uehara set down the first two batters in the bottom of the frame, but the third hitter, Jose Lobaton — filling in after Wil Myers left with leg cramps — played hero. The part-time catcher sent a walk-off solo shot into the Touch Tank in right-center, keeping Tampa Bay's season alive for one more day.

	1	2	3	4	5	6	7	8	9	R	H	E
BOSTON	1	0	0	0	2	0	0	0	1	4	7	0
TAMPA BAY	0	0	0	0	3	0	0	1	1	5	11	1

WP: Rodney LP: Uehara
HR: TB: Longoria, Lobaton

Buchholz was solid through six and got a 3-0 lead from his offense, but it wasn't enough to hold down the Rays, who scored three off the righty.

"THE RAYS REALLY DO A NICE JOB OF PUTTING THE BALL IN PLAY AND MAKING THE MOST OUT OF THE OPPORTUNITIES THEY HAVE. THEY JUST HAVE SUCH A GOOD MENTALITY AS A TEAM. THEY GRIND IT OUT. THEY ARE NEVER OUT OF IT." Jake Peavy

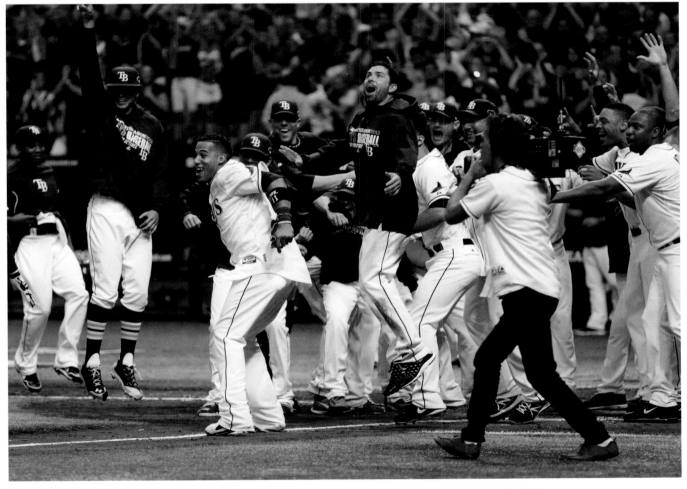

The Rays were ecstatic when Lobaton went deep in the bottom of the ninth, tightening the series gap with a walk-off blast.

GAME 4, OCT. 8
RED SOX 3, RAYS 1

IT TOOK BEANTOWN FOUR YEARS OF TRIAL AND tribulation to return to the postseason, but it took just five days for the Red Sox to dispatch the Rays and secure the franchise's 10th League Championship Series berth.

Rays skipper Joe Maddon gave starter Jeremy Hellickson the early hook after he loaded the bases to lead off the second inning, but Tampa Bay escaped when first baseman James Loney engineered a stunning 3-6 double play after snagging a high liner. Boston starter Jake Peavy remained steady through five innings as the pitching carousel continued for Tampa (nine hurlers saw action).

The score remained locked at zero until the Rays' David DeJesus broke through with an RBI single in the sixth. The Red Sox responded in the next inning, though, as rookie Xander Bogaerts tied the game when he scored on a wild pitch by Joel Peralta. Shane Victorino drove in Jacoby Ellsbury for the go-ahead run two pitches later. Thanks to the stellar bullpen triumvirate of Craig Breslow, Junichi Tazawa and Koji Uehara (3.1 innings pitched, 1 hit, 0 runs combined), Boston held on to advance.

	1	2	3	4	5	6	7	8	9	R	H	E
BOSTON	0	0	0	0	0	0	2	0	1	3	6	0
TAMPA BAY	0	0	0	0	0	1	0	0	0	1	6	0

WP: Breslow LP: McGee SV: Uehara

Ellsbury (left) singled and stole second before scoring on Victorino's seventh-inning knock. The 38-year-old Uehara recorded his second career postseason save to send the Red Sox to the American League Championship Series.

Victorino, who joined the Red Sox before the season, drove in the go-ahead run in the clincher.

"WE KNEW IT WAS GOING TO BE A TOUGH SERIES. THIS IS THE PART OF BASEBALL THAT YOU LOOK FORWARD TO AND TRAIN FOR EVERY OFFSEASON. WE HAVE TWO MORE [SERIES] TO GO, BUT IT'S ALWAYS NICE TO BE ABLE TO MOVE ON." Shane Victorino

GAME 4, OCT. 8
RED SOX 3, RAYS 1

"WE KNEW THIS WASN'T GOING TO BE A SIMPLE SERIES. WE WERE ABLE TO WIN TWO GAMES AT HOME AND COME DOWN HERE NEEDING TO WIN JUST ONE. THIS IS NOT A FRIENDLY PLACE TO PLAY. WE'RE FORTUNATE NOT TO GO ALL FIVE GAMES." Craig Breslow

GAME 1, OCT. 12
TIGERS 1, RED SOX 0

THE TIGERS PITCHED THEMSELVES TO THE DOORSTEP of history as Anibal Sanchez and four relievers carried a no-hitter into the ninth inning at Fenway Park, bidding for just the third no-no in MLB postseason history.

Despite not allowing a hit and striking out 12, Sanchez labored through six innings, walking six batters. He got the hook before the seventh and passed the torch to Al Alburquerque, Jose Veras and Drew Smyly in succession, who combined to retire Boston in order over the next two innings.

Staked to a 1-0 lead thanks to Jhonny Peralta's RBI single in the sixth, Detroit brought in closer Joaquin Benoit to seal the victory and possibly history. The latter slipped away when Daniel Nava blooped a one-out single, but the former stayed intact. Boston's lineup, which whiffed 17 times and went 0 for 6 with runners in scoring position, could not push a run across.

	1	2	3	4	5	6	7	8	9	R	H	E
DETROIT	0	0	0	0	0	1	0	0	0	1	9	0
BOSTON	0	0	0	0	0	0	0	0	0	0	1	1

WP: Sanchez **LP:** Lester **SV:** Benoit

Jon Lester pitched 6.1 innings of six-hit, one-run ball in Game 1, but took the hard-luck loss against Detroit's near-no-hitter.

"I THINK WE'LL BE READY TO GO TOMORROW NIGHT. IF YOU HAVEN'T BEEN AROUND US THIS YEAR, WE HAVE THE ABILITY TO PUT THINGS BEHIND US. WE'LL BE READY TO GO."
John Farrell

The Red Sox's lineup went hitless until Nava stroked a single off Tigers closer Benoit with one out in the ninth inning.

GAME 2, OCT. 13
RED SOX 6, TIGERS 5

ALREADY 2-0 IN THE 2013 POSTSEASON, MAX SCHERZER took the mound and kept the K party going for the Tigers, striking out 13 and allowing just two hits and two walks over seven innings. The Detroit offense awoke after a relatively dormant Game 1 with eight hits and five earned runs against Clay Buchholz, including a solo homer by Miguel Cabrera and a two-run shot by Alex Avila, both in the sixth.

But David Ortiz, who's been known to turn the tide of a game or two in October, knotted it up at five with a dramatic two-out grand slam in the eighth inning. Big Papi launched the first pitch he saw from Tigers closer Joaquin Benoit to right-center field, and it sailed just out of reach of Torii Hunter, who tumbled over the low wall while attempting the catch.

The Red Sox's bullpen had long since stopped the bleeding, holding Detroit hitless over the last 3.1 innings and setting the stage for a dramatic ninth, in which Jarrod Saltalamacchia drove in Jonny Gomes — who led off the inning with a single — to complete the comeback and even the series.

	1	2	3	4	5	6	7	8	9	R	H	E
DETROIT	0	1	0	0	0	4	0	0	0	5	8	1
BOSTON	0	0	0	0	0	1	0	4	1	6	7	1

WP: Uehara **LP**: Porcello
HR: DET: Cabrera, Avila; BOS: Ortiz

In the iconic shot of the 2013 postseason, Boston police officer Steve Horgan celebrated with fans as Ortiz's home run sailed past a diving Hunter.

"I KNOW THEY'RE NOT GOING TO LET ME BEAT THEM ON A FASTBALL IN THAT SITUATION. MY BOY BENOIT HAS A GOOD SPLITTER AND I TOOK MY CHANCES. BUT THAT PITCH WAS ON THE PLATE AND I PUT A GOOD SWING ON IT." David Ortiz

Ortiz (left) was greeted by Dustin Pedroia (center) and Will Middlebrooks after he drove them in with his game-tying grand slam.

GAME 2, OCT. 13
RED SOX 6, TIGERS 5

On a 3-1 count, Saltalamacchia hit a sharp single to left, scoring Gomes and evening the series at one game apiece.

"I TRIED BUNTING AGAINST THEM EARLIER IN THE YEAR AND IT DIDN'T WORK OUT SO WELL. I FIGURED I'D GO AHEAD AND SWING THE BAT, AND I FELT GOOD." Jarrod Saltalamacchia

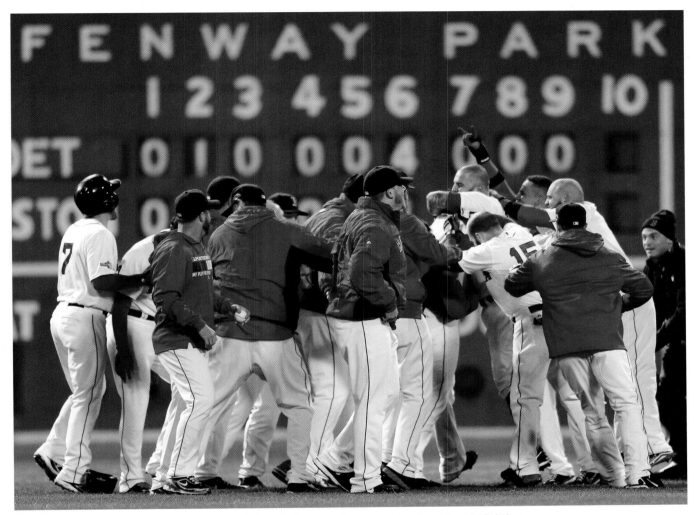

The Red Sox celebrated in front of their home crowd after winning Game 2, sending the series to Detroit all tied up.

PAPI'S GREATEST HITS

FEW, IF ANY, players in Major League history have shared David Ortiz's ability to come up big in high-pressure October situations. Big Papi once again flexed his clutch muscles in Game 2 with a game-tying grand slam in the eighth inning, but it was just one critical hit in his robust collection of season-altering at-bats.

His legend began in the 2004 ALDS with a walk-off home run in the 10th inning of Game 3, which completed a sweep of the Angels and propelled Boston to its now-legendary ALCS against New York. It was in that ensuing series that Ortiz provided his two most iconic postseason at-bats: a 12th-inning walk-off homer in Game 4 and a 14th-inning walk-off single in Game 5, staving off near-certain elimination and catalyzing a miraculous 3-games-to-none comeback en route to Boston's first title in 86 years.

GAME 3, OCT. 15
RED SOX 1, TIGERS 0

THE SECOND-INNING POWER OUTAGE AT COMERICA Park that briefly delayed Game 3 served as proper foreshadowing for the afternoon. Both lineups fell prey to lights-out starting pitching, as Boston's John Lackey and Detroit's Justin Verlander combined to give up just eight hits and strike out 18 over 14.2 total innings.

But something had to give, and in the top of the seventh, Mike Napoli — who hit a home run off the Tigers' ace in his first career at-bat in 2006 — drove a 3-2 four-seamer from Verlander over the left-field fence. Despite his eight innings of 10-strikeout, four-hit ball, Verlander's lone blemish would cost the Tigers, as the Boston's pitching did not give the Detroit lineup an inch.

Lackey struck out eight over 6.2 innings before reluctantly handing the ball to the familiar bullpen trio of Craig Breslow, Junichi Tazawa and Koji Uehara in succession, the last of whom tossed a four-out save to preserve the 1-0 win.

	1	2	3	4	5	6	7	8	9	R	H	E
BOSTON	0	0	0	0	0	0	1	0	0	1	4	0
DETROIT	0	0	0	0	0	0	0	0	0	0	6	1

WP: Lackey LP: Verlander SV: Uehara
HR: BOS: Napoli

Lackey went toe-to-toe with Verlander and outdueled the former MVP, whiffing eight batters over 6.2 scoreless frames.

As per tradition, backup catcher David Ross (left) tugged on Napoli's beard after the first baseman hit a solo homer for the game's only run.

"EVERY GAME IS BIG. YOU COME OUT AND YOU PREPARE. YOU GET A GAME PLAN. EVERY PLAYOFF GAME IS DIFFERENT. WHATEVER THE SITUATION IS, YOU'VE GOT TO TRY TO EXECUTE." Mike Napoli

GAME 3, OCT. 15
RED SOX 1, TIGERS 0

For his part, Verlander was excellent in Game 3, going eight full innings, striking out 10 and allowing just one run.

Jarrod Saltalamacchia (left) congratulated Uehara after Boston's closer converted a high-pressure, four-out save.

"I WOULDN'T SAY IT'S FRUSTRATING. I THINK YOU KIND OF EXPECT THAT IN THIS SERIES. IT'S GOING TO BE A BATTLE FOR EVERY SINGLE OUT, EVERY SINGLE RUN — IT'S TWO HEAVYWEIGHTS GOING AT IT. IF YOU CAN'T APPRECIATE THIS, YOU CAN'T APPRECIATE BASEBALL. TOUGH ONE TODAY, BUT WE'LL BOUNCE BACK LIKE WE HAVE ALL YEAR."
Justin Verlander

GAME 4, OCT. 16
TIGERS 7, RED SOX 3

JIM LEYLAND'S LINEUP CARD SEEMED PUZZLING AT first, with Torii Hunter in the leadoff spot, Miguel Cabrera batting second and Austin Jackson in the eight-hole. But his new-look order paid off in spades, as Detroit topped its combined run output from Games 1–3, evening the series with a 7-3 romp.

Ahead 1-0 in the second, the Tigers opened the floodgates with a two-out, four-run rally after Dustin Pedroia misplayed a possible inning-ending double-play ball. With runners on the corners, Hunter smashed a bases-clearing double and subsequently scored on a Cabrera single. Jackson and Cabrera followed with RBI singles in the fourth, as all seven runs were charged to Red Sox starter Jake Peavy.

Boston matched its combined hit output from the first three games with 12 base knocks, but Detroit starter Doug Fister allowed just one run and struck out seven over six solid innings, earning his first win of the 2013 postseason.

	1	2	3	4	5	6	7	8	9	R	H	E
BOSTON	0	0	0	0	0	1	1	0	1	3	12	0
DETROIT	0	5	0	2	0	0	0	0	x	7	9	0

WP: Fister **LP:** Peavy

Peavy did not bring his best stuff in Game 4, allowing seven earned runs against a reshuffled and reenergized Tigers lineup.

Jackson benefitted from his new spot in the order, going 2 for 2 with two walks and two RBI, reaching base in each of his plate appearances.

"IT FELT A LITTLE DIFFERENT HITTING DOWN IN THE ORDER AND COMING UP AFTER GUYS HAD ALREADY HIT. I THINK THAT IT DEFINITELY HELPED TO BE ABLE TO GET TO SEE SOME OF THE PITCHES THAT [PEAVY] WAS THROWING AND HAVE A GAME PLAN."
Austin Jackson

GAME 5, OCT. 17
RED SOX 4, TIGERS 3

MIKE NAPOLI PAVED THE WAY FOR A RED SOX VICTORY in a pivotal Game 5 by going 3 for 4 with two RBI — including a tone-setting, 460-foot moonshot to center field in the second inning.

Detroit starter Anibal Sanchez struggled early, allowing two more runs in the second and one in the third. Red Sox catcher David Ross started in place of Jarrod Saltalamacchia and found himself in the thick of two critical plays early on, one in which he tagged out Miguel Cabrera at the plate in the first, the next in which he was tagged out in a collision with Tigers catcher Alex Avila an inning later. Also making a notable start was 21-year-old Xander Bogaerts, who scored on a Ross double.

The Red Sox almost squandered their 4-0 lead as Detroit tacked on a run in the fifth, sixth and seventh innings. But closer Koji Uehara came on with one out in the eighth and set down five Tigers in succession, sending the series back to Boston with a 3-games-to-2 advantage.

	1	2	3	4	5	6	7	8	9	R	H	E
BOSTON	0	3	1	0	0	0	0	0	0	4	10	0
DETROIT	0	0	0	0	1	1	1	0	0	3	10	1

WP: Lester **LP:** Sanchez **SV:** Uehara
HR: BOS: Napoli

Starting in Game 5, Ross laced an RBI double to left in the second inning, but was thrown out at the plate two batters later.

"IT'S BEEN A CRAZY YEAR. I'M 21 AND STARTED [THE SEASON] IN DOUBLE-A; NOW I'M HERE IN THE ALCS, ONE GAME AWAY FROM THE WORLD SERIES. SOMETIMES IT'S HARD TO BELIEVE."
Xander Bogaerts

Jacoby Ellsbury followed Ross's double with a single of his own, scoring Bogaerts and giving Boston an early 3-0 lead.

GAME 5, OCT. 17
RED SOX 4, TIGERS 3

Uehara rose to the occasion once again in Game 5, striking out Jhonny Peralta and Omar Infante in the eighth before sealing the win with a 1-2-3 ninth.

Napoli followed his home run with a ground-rule double the next inning and scored Boston's fourth run — the game-winner — on a wild pitch.

"HE'S PICKED US UP IN BIG SITUATIONS THROUGHOUT THE SEASON. TONIGHT WAS ANOTHER ONE OF THOSE SITUATIONS, PUTTING US UP 1-0 OFF A PRETTY GOOD PITCHER. IT'S A BIG PARK AND HE MADE THE YARD LOOK SMALL WITH THAT SWING."

Jon Lester on Mike Napoli

GAME 6, OCT. 19
RED SOX 5, TIGERS 2

IN A SERIES THAT SO OFTEN HINGED ON THE LONGBALL, it was appropriate that Boston's final offensive push for a spot in the Fall Classic came courtesy of another thrilling late-inning grand slam.

The dramatics were provided by Shane Victorino, who had gone 2 for 21 in the first five games of the ALCS. With his team down 2-1 with one out and the bases loaded in the seventh, Victorino sent a hanging curveball from Jose Veras soaring over the Green Monster, plating Jonny Gomes, Xander Bogaerts and Jacoby Ellsbury. The grand slam spoiled a solid effort from Tigers starter Max Scherzer, who had exited the game with the lead.

Par for the course, the Red Sox bullpen stifled the Tigers in the late innings. ALCS MVP Koji Uehara struck out Jose Iglesias to earn his third save of the series and secure the Red Sox's 12th American League pennant.

	1	2	3	4	5	6	7	8	9	R	H	E
DETROIT	0	0	0	0	0	2	0	0	0	2	8	1
BOSTON	0	0	0	0	1	0	4	0	x	5	5	1

WP: Tazawa **LP**: Scherzer **SV**: Uehara
HR: BOS: Victorino

Down 2-1 with the bases loaded in the seventh, Victorino sent a grand slam over the Green Monster, putting the Red Sox ahead for good.

"LAST YEAR, PEOPLE SAID I WAS DONE. BUT WHEN I CAME HERE, THERE WAS *REJUBILATION*. THERE WAS SOMETHING INSIDE OF ME THAT SAID, 'I WANT TO PROVE SOMETHING.'" Shane Victorino

From left: Dustin Pedroia greeted Gomes and Bogaerts as they crossed the plate on Victorino's grand slam.

GAME 6, OCT. 19
RED SOX 5, TIGERS 2

ALCS MVP Uehara was mobbed by his teammates after striking out former Red Sox shortstop Iglesias for the final out of the series.

Gomes embraced the clubhouse celebration after the Red Sox clinched their 12th American League pennant and third in 10 seasons.

U DID IT

AMONG THE MID-LEVEL free-agent signings that panned out so marvelously for the Red Sox in 2013, perhaps none were less heralded — or yielded the kind of extraordinary results — than the addition of Koji Uehara. Inked to a one-year, $4.25-million deal, the journeyman reliever went from seventh-inning bullpen option to ALCS MVP, authoring one of the finest stretches of relief pitching Major League Baseball has ever seen.

After first-string closer Joel Hanrahan went down with an elbow injury and backup Andrew Bailey fell prey to shoulder issues, Uehara stepped into the closer's role and shined. He saved 21 games in 24 opportunities, did not allow a run over a nearly two-month stretch, and posted a 0.565 WHIP that was the lowest single-season mark of all time (min. 50 IP).

Always trying to rally his teammates with a timely high-five, Uehara propelled the Red Sox from both the mound and the dugout — all the way to a World Series title.

GAME 1, OCT. 23
RED SOX 8, CARDINALS 1

THE RED SOX FORMED AN IDENTITY IN 2013 CENTERED on their many styles of beards, but it was the Cardinals for whom things got hairy in Game 1. St. Louis prides itself on playing "The Cardinal Way" — which generally means mistake-free baseball — but an uncharacteristic three errors and lack of command from ace Adam Wainwright set the tone early, and the Red Sox capitalized. Once umpires overturned a first-inning call on a potential double-play ball dropped by shortstop Pete Kozma, the Sox had the Cards on the ropes with the bases loaded and one out. Mike Napoli made them pay immediately, lacing a three-run double into the left-center-field gap to stake Boston to a 3-0 lead.

It was an all-too-familiar sight for St. Louis — as Napoli, a member of the Rangers in the 2011 World Series, batted .350 with two home runs and 10 RBI against the Cardinals. As a team, the Red Sox also picked up where they left off in World Series play, extending their Fall Classic winning streak to nine. The starting pitcher on the mound for win No. 8, which came in Game 4 of the 2007 World Series against the Colorado Rockies, was fittingly Jon Lester. The big left-hander stifled a loaded Cardinals lineup on this night, striking out eight in 7.2 scoreless innings. "Lester just kept pounding the zone," Red Sox left fielder Jonny Gomes said. "He's got such composure — when he had the bases loaded and one out (in the fourth inning), he kept his cool."

Lester's dominance and the breaks the Cardinals provided with lackluster defense — in the second, Wainwright called for a pop-up, but let it land between him and catcher Yadier Molina — was plenty to propel Boston to its lopsided victory. Team spark plug Dustin Pedroia had two hits, while David Ortiz collected a single, home run and three RBI, and was also robbed of a grand slam on a dynamite play by Carlos Beltran, who reached over the right-field wall to make the catch. Unfortunately, even that Redbirds highlight had a downside, as Beltran left the game with a bruised rib, and the Red Sox cruised to an 8-1 win.

	1	2	3	4	5	6	7	8	9	R	H	E
ST. LOUIS	0	0	0	0	0	0	0	0	1	1	7	3
BOSTON	3	2	0	0	0	0	2	1	x	8	8	1

WP: Lester LP: Wainwright
HR: STL: Holliday; BOS: Ortiz

Napoli fired the first shot of the Fall Classic, capitalizing on Kozma's error by ripping a three-run double into the left-center-field gap.

Lester was in ace form in Game 1, pitching 7.2 shutout innings, allowing just five hits, walking one and striking out eight.

GAME 1, OCT. 23
RED SOX 8, CARDINALS 1

"BEING AT HOME HELPS AMP EVERYTHING UP. THE BIGGEST THING IS BEING ABLE TO CONTROL THOSE EMOTIONS AND PITCH UNDER CONTROL — JUST RELY ON LOCATION EARLY ON, TRY TO GET INTO A RHYTHM AND GET YOUR LEGS UNDER YOU. WE WERE ABLE TO DO THAT IN THE FIRST INNING AND WENT FROM THERE." Jon Lester

One of two pitchers remaining from the 2007 championship team, Lester saluted the jubilant Fenway Park crowd after his sterling performance in Game 1; Ortiz (right) sent the stadium into a frenzy with a two-run insurance blast in the seventh, scoring Pedroia.

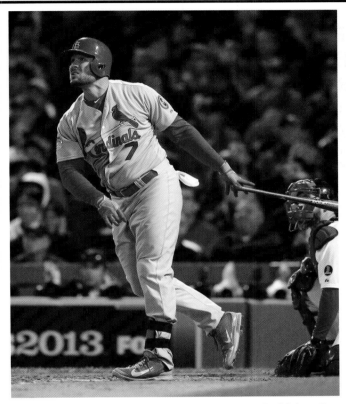

Cardinals left fielder Matt Holliday (above) finally put the Redbirds on the board with a solo home run in the ninth inning. Beltran, playing in the first World Series game of his 16-year career, robbed Ortiz of a grand slam in the second inning, but sustained a game-ending rib injury on the play.

REVERSAL OF FORTUNE

ALTHOUGH THE SERIES had just begun, one play in the bottom of the first inning at Fenway Park immediately stood out as one of its defining moments. The Red Sox stormed to a decisive victory on a brisk night in Boston, but the tide of events could have been much different.

With runners on first and second, David Ortiz hit an easy grounder to second baseman Matt Carpenter. Thinking double play off the bat, Carpenter flipped to shortstop Pete Kozma, who watched the ball bounce off the tip of his glove. Umpire Dana DeMuth ruled runner Dustin Pedroia out on the play, claiming Kozma had dropped the ball during the transfer. But replays showed otherwise, and the umpiring crew got together to overturn the call, ruling that he never had possession — a virtually unprecedented, albeit correct, decision.

The reversal sparked a rally, as Mike Napoli subsequently knocked a bases-clearing double to put the Sox ahead. They never looked back. "If we turn that double play, it's going to be different," said Cardinals backstop Yadier Molina. "[But] it was a good call. You want the call to be right."

GAME 2, OCT. 24
CARDINALS 4, RED SOX 2

WITH CARLOS BELTRAN'S BAT BACK IN THE LINEUP and Michael Wacha's blazing arm on the mound for the fourth time this postseason, the Cardinals were poised to avenge the previous night's defeat from the moment Game 2 started. And when they got on the board first, courtesy of a Matt Holliday triple and Yadier Molina RBI in the fourth — after Wacha had held the Sox to just one hit — St. Louis had imprinted its stamp on the game.

Beltran, 36, and Wacha, 22, were both experiencing the World Series for the first time in their vastly different careers. But their paths converged, as the young, postseason-tested hurler whiffed six in as many innings of work and the veteran slugger knocked two hits a day after leaving Game 1 early with a bruised rib. "The guy's obviously banged up after running into the wall," said infielder Daniel Descalso. "He battled through the pain and came out and got two big hits for us tonight — drove in a nice insurance run. It was nice to have him in the lineup."

The Cards' starter wasn't fazed on the road, despite the taunting chants of "Waaa-chaaa" that echoed throughout Fenway whenever he found himself in a tough spot.

"Nerves weren't too bad — [I was] just anxious to get out there," he said. "It's the World Series, a big-time game. I tried to use it to my advantage and pitch with some adrenaline, and just try to block out the fans and the crowd."

His lone blip on the night was a hanging change-up that yielded yet another mammoth two-run homer by David Ortiz — into the first row of the Green Monster — who made the rookie pay for the free pass he issued to Dustin Pedroia the batter prior. But St. Louis's other young studs came in for some spotless relief work, as Carlos Martinez and Trevor Rosenthal allowed just one base runner combined.

And in the bottom of the seventh, the Cardinals got the boost they had been waiting for: A Matt Carpenter sac fly with the bases loaded induced a sequence of Sox miscues, as a pair of errors allowed an additional run to score. Beltran then followed with a single that drove in an extra run for good measure, ensuring that the Cardinals would take the Series home on equal footing.

	1	2	3	4	5	6	7	8	9	R	H	E
ST. LOUIS	0	0	0	1	0	0	3	0	0	4	7	1
BOSTON	0	0	0	0	0	2	0	0	0	2	4	2

WP: Wacha LP: Lackey SV: Rosenthal
HR: BOS: Ortiz

The energy at Fenway Park was palpable for Game 2, as 38,436 fans watched the Red Sox take on the Cards.

Ortiz hit his second home run in as many World Series games with a two-run blast in the sixth, the 17th of his postseason career.

"LOSING THE GAME IS FRUSTRATING, FOR SURE. I FELT GOOD TONIGHT. I PROBABLY HAD A LITTLE BETTER FAST-BALL THAN MY LAST START. BUT THEIR GUY WAS PITCHING WELL. THE MARGIN FOR ERROR IS REALLY SLIM THIS TIME OF YEAR. [WE] KIND OF LET ONE GO, BUT WE'LL BE BACK FOR THE NEXT ONE." John Lackey

GAME 2, OCT. 24
CARDINALS 4, RED SOX 2

Clockwise from top left: Massachusetts native James Taylor, along with his wife Kim and son Henry, sang "America the Beautiful" during the seventh-inning stretch. Among those honored on the field were families of the fallen from the Boston Marathon tragedy, as well as those injured in the attacks — some of whom were walking in public for the first time since April — and heroes who saved others. Fans bundled up on a chilly night in Boston for Game 2, only to see their team fall short, as St. Louis scored the go-ahead run on a throwing error by reliever Craig Breslow in the seventh.

THE OLD AND THE NEW

THE CARDINALS AND the Red Sox both entered the World Series with the best record (97-65) in their respective leagues. But while St. Louis placed rookies and second-year players in huge roles all season long – and it was never more prevalent than in October, when 22-year-old Michael Wacha and 25-year-old Joe Kelly formed half of its postseason rotation – Boston in contrast was led by big-character, uber-experienced veterans like Mike Napoli, Shane Victorino and David Ortiz.

After his Game 2 grand slam turned the tide of the ALCS, Ortiz just kept raking, launching a home run in both Games 1 and 2 of the World Series – a sight baseball fans have come to expect from Big Papi – bringing his 2013 postseason total to five.

For Cardinals Game 2 starter Wacha, who was drafted out of Texas A&M less than 17 months prior, each postseason assignment posed a greater challenge than the previous start. By the time he faced the Red Sox, many wondered how he'd fare against a deep and patient American League lineup. He responded by doing what he did to the Pirates and Dodgers before – keeping hitters off balance and overpowering them with the hard stuff.

With the Game 2 victory, Wacha improved his postseason record to 4-0 during a month some Redbird followers dubbed "Wach-tober." He strung together a scoreless streak of 19 innings before the home run by that experienced guy, Ortiz, in the sixth.

GAME 3, OCT. 26
CARDINALS 5, RED SOX 4

FALL CLASSIC HISTORY IS FILLED WITH INDIVIDUAL plays that define an iconic game, like Fred Snodgrass's Muff, Carlton Fisk's Wave-it-Fair Shot or Kirk Gibson's Hobbling Homer. Enter a new title: The Obstruction.

Part of the beauty of baseball is that no matter how many games have been staged, there's always a play or a situation that seems brand new. Sure, obstruction has been called plenty of times, all the way down to the Little League level, but never has it *ended* a World Series game.

Jon Jay came to the plate in the bottom of the ninth with one out, runners on second and third, recently unhittable Koji Uehara on the mound and the score tied, 4-4. He laced a two-hopper that second baseman Dustin Pedroia dove to backhand for a spectacular grab, then fired a strike home to nail Yadier Molina for the second out. When Allen Craig decided to break for third, catcher Jarrod Saltal- amacchia tried to throw him out, but instead fired the ball past third baseman Will Middlebrooks and into left field. Craig — hobbled by a re-aggravation of his earlier foot injury — struggled to get up, tripping over Middle- brooks, who was lying flat on the ground, and stumbling home. Left fielder Daniel Nava fielded the overthrow and fired a perfect pea home to beat Craig by several steps, but

third base umpire Jim Joyce had already called obstruction on Middlebrooks, and Craig was awarded home.

"At the time, I had no idea what happened," Cardinals outfielder Carlos Beltran said. "Maybe 75 percent of the guys on the field didn't know what had happened. All I knew was that we won."

Leading up to the unbelievable finish, Game 3 provided thrills throughout as the pendulum swung back and forth. Matt Holliday's two-run double in the seventh gave the Cards a 4-2 lead, but Sox youngster Xander Bogaerts' two-out RBI single in the eighth capped a two-run rally to tie the score. The Redbirds won the battle of bullpens when closer Trevor Rosenthal tossed 1.2 innings of one-hit ball to set the stage for the game-ending theatrics. So many amazing pieces of this puzzle will be lost to history, but the final one — *The Obstruction* — will be remembered for all time.

	1	2	3	4	5	6	7	8	9	R	H	E
BOSTON	0	0	0	0	1	1	0	2	0	4	6	2
ST. LOUIS	2	0	0	0	0	0	2	0	1	5	12	0

WP: Rosenthal **LP:** Workman

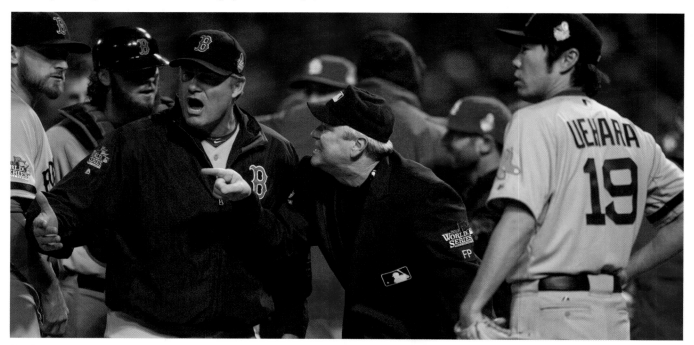

Red Sox Manager John Farrell (left) and home plate umpire Dana DeMuth (center) exchanged words over the unprecedented call.

DeMuth immediately ruled Craig safe at home, signalling that third base ump Joyce had already called obstruction.

MLB RULE 7.06 STATES: "IF A PLAY IS BEING MADE ON THE OBSTRUCTED RUNNER … THE BALL IS DEAD AND ALL RUNNERS SHALL ADVANCE, WITHOUT LIABILITY TO BE PUT OUT, TO THE BASES THEY WOULD HAVE REACHED, IN THE UMPIRE'S JUDGMENT, IF THERE HAD BEEN NO OBSTRUCTION. THE OBSTRUCTED RUNNER SHALL BE AWARDED AT LEAST ONE BASE BEYOND THE BASE HE HAD LAST LEGALLY TOUCHED."

GAME 3, OCT. 26
CARDINALS 5, RED SOX 4

The scene around home plate at the end of the game was equal parts confusion and celebration, as the Cardinals took a 2-games-to-1 Series lead.

"YOU DON'T WANT TO LOSE. BUT IF THE RULEBOOK SAYS THAT'S OBSTRUCTION, THEN YOU TIP YOUR HAT, WALK OFF THE FIELD, AND TAKE IT LIKE A MAN." Jarrod Saltalamacchia

With two on and nobody out in the seventh, Holliday (left) broke a 2-2 tie with a two-run double to left. David Ortiz played first base just six times during the regular season, but manned the position in Game 3 as the Red Sox were without a designated hitter in the National League park.

Bogaerts went 2 for 4 with an RBI, including a fifth-inning triple on which he scored three batters later.

'PEN IS MIGHTIER

IN A SERIES defined by dominant moundsmen in the first two games, Game 3 was a bit of a break from character. While Boston veteran Jake Peavy was looking to avenge his less-than-memorable performance in the ALCS – in which he surrendered seven runs in just three innings in a loss to the Tigers – young St. Louis fireballer Joe Kelly was out to continue the solid work he had done in 16.1 previous innings this postseason. But the starters lasted just four and 5.1 innings respectively, and their jobs were turned over to a pair of stellar bullpens.

Manager John Farrell called on Felix Doubront, normally a starter, for long relief work, and the left-hander threw two scoreless innings before handing the ball over to the Red Sox's regular late-game crew. "[Doubront] hasn't pitched in over a week. For him to come in like that and pitch as well as he did, you can't be anything but happy with that effort," said batterymate Jarrod Saltalamacchia.

Craig Breslow, Junichi Tazawa, Brandon Workman and Koji Uehara – whom Farrell intended to use for two innings – followed, but the normally lights-out contingent (all but Breslow had a 0.00 ERA through three games, while Uehara led the pack with a 0.75 WHIP) allowed a single and a double to the heart of the Cards' lineup before the controversial obstruction call foiled their efforts.

GAME 4, OCT. 27
RED SOX 4, CARDINALS 2

WHEN GAME 3 ENDED ON AN OBSTRUCTION CALL with two outs in the bottom of the ninth, it seemed as if the World Series quirks quota had been reached. But Game 4 checked off another box on the strange finish spectrum: the first-ever World Series contest to end on a pickoff.

A night after he scored the winning run after tripping over Sox third baseman Will Middlebrooks while running home, pinch-hitter Allen Craig knocked a ninth-inning single off the right-field wall to keep the Cardinals' hopes alive with a 4-2 deficit. Kolten Wong promptly took his spot as a pinch-runner, but the game ended abruptly with Carlos Beltran at the plate, as Boston closer Koji Uehara caught Wong leaning toward second and threw behind him to secure the final out — and tie the series.

The muscle of the night came from the heart of Boston's lineup. While the Cardinals got on the board in the bottom of the third — this was the first 2013 postseason game in which the Cards scored the first run and did not win — David Ortiz, the DH-turned–first baseman in this NL park, doubled to lead off the fifth and came around to score on Stephen Drew's sac fly.

"That guy leads by example," said Boston's Game 4 catcher David Ross. "Their attack on him — what they call when he comes to the plate — is totally different. They're saying, 'We're not going to let David Ortiz beat us with Jonny [Gomes] or [Daniel] Nava behind him.'"

It was Gomes who batted fifth on this night, and unfortunately for the Cards, both he and Ortiz did some damage in the sixth, when Dustin Pedroia started a two-out rally with a single before Ortiz walked. Seth Maness came in to relieve starter Lance Lynn, but the change failed to slow Boston down, as Gomes launched a 2-2 pitch over the fence in deep left-center. The blast would prove to be the difference-maker in the game, courtesy of a man who didn't even know he was starting the game in place of usual right fielder Shane Victorino (sore back) until batting practice.

"It couldn't happen to anybody better than Jonny," said starter Clay Buchholz, who allowed one unearned run in four innings of work. "He wants to play every day, but when he's not in the lineup, he takes it and is ready for whenever John [Farrell] calls his name. "

	1	2	3	4	5	6	7	8	9	R	H	E
BOSTON	0	0	0	0	1	3	0	0	0	4	6	2
ST. LOUIS	0	0	1	0	0	0	1	0	0	2	6	0

WP: Doubront **LP:** Lynn **SV:** Uehara
HR: BOS: Gomes

Mike Napoli, a defensive substitute at first base, tagged out Wong for the last out of Game 4 with Beltran — the potential tying run — at the plate.

Clockwise from top: Gomes watched as his three-run homer sailed over the left-field fence, and was soon greeted by his elated teammates; Uehara and Napoli high-fived after teaming up to pick off Wong and end the game.

GAME 4, OCT. 27
RED SOX 4, CARDINALS 2

Ortiz proved to be by far the toughest out in the Red Sox's lineup, going all-out for his third ring. Through four World Series games, Big Papi was batting .727 (including a 3-for-3 effort in Game 4), reaching base at a .750 clip and posting an inconceivable 1.364 slugging percentage.

"AS ONE OF THE OLDER PLAYERS, I WATCH THINGS. I JUST WANT TO GET EVERYBODY IN THE MOOD. I LET EVERYBODY KNOW, 'LET'S LOOSEN UP AND PLAY THE GAME THE WAY WE NORMALLY DO.'" David Ortiz

Cardinals leadoff man Matt Carpenter (above) accounted for both St. Louis runs, scoring in the third and driving in Shane Robinson with a single in the seventh, while Buchholz limited the Redbirds to one unearned run on three hits in four innings.

HERE'S JONNY

ENTERING GAME 4, Jonny Gomes was 0 for 8 at the plate in the Series and didn't even expect to play. But while warming up for his assumed bench role, he received the news that Shane Victorino had a tight back and that he would be starting in Victorino's place. He also drew the fifth spot in the batting order, meaning he had to protect the red-hot David Ortiz.

As he has done all season long, Gomes found ways to create a spark for Boston with his fiery personality and willingness to throw himself around the field. "He's been one of our leaders in the clubhouse," said Manager John Farrell. "His importance to this team goes above and beyond the numbers he puts up."

He didn't make things look nearly as smooth in the outfield as Victorino likely would have, but he ultimately made all the requisite plays. At the plate, he drove Cardinals pitchers batty, seeing 23 total pitches in Game 4, drawing two walks and, most importantly, delivering the game's decisive blow. With two men on and two outs in a 1-1, sixth-inning tie, Gomes greeted reliever Seth Maness with a three-run homer to put the Red Sox ahead to stay.

GAME 5, OCT. 28
RED SOX 3, CARDINALS 1

IF ANY DOUBTS LINGERED ABOUT WHETHER JON Lester needed some sneaky help in his dazzling Game 1 performance, the big left-hander put those thoughts to rest in Game 5. Just days after cameras picked up a greenish substance in his glove that apparently helped him grip the ball in cold weather, Lester took the hill again, this time with temperatures near 50 degrees, and he was just as dominant with no signs of trickery. He outdueled Cards ace Adam Wainwright — who fanned 10 batters in seven solid innings — allowing just one run in 7.2 frames

Lester (top) entered rarefied air in Game 5, becoming just the second Red Sox southpaw — joining Babe Ruth — to win three World Series games. Dustin Pedroia scored the first run of the game on an Ortiz double.

while striking out seven and walking none. The lone blemish of his night was a mammoth home run by Matt Holliday in the fourth inning. Lester earned his second win of the World Series and improved to 4-1 with a 1.56 ERA this postseason, allowing two earned runs or less in each of his October starts.

"Unbelievable," said teammate David Ortiz. "Jon is a guy who comes through, especially in games like that. He brought everything he had. He knows how to do it."

Big Papi also knows how to do it in the World Series. Ortiz put the Red Sox on the board first with an RBI double in the first inning and collected three hits on the night. When he singled in the fourth, it marked his ninth straight World Series plate appearance in which he reached base safely, tying a Fall Classic record. "I was born for this," Ortiz said after the game. He also had reached base in all 13 career Fall Classic games dating back to 2004, and his 2013 World Series average jumped to an astonishing .733 by the end of Game 5.

"He's incredible," said teammate Stephen Drew. "He's a great hitter — everyone knows that. The thing about him is he doesn't miss his pitch when he gets it."

Boston finished the game with a lowly .226 team World Series batting average and a postseason-record 150 strikeouts. But history told them that the 1918 Red Sox — the last club to win a World Series clincher at Fenway Park — batted just .186, and through five games this time around, the key hits came just often enough. Catcher David Ross laced a ground-rule, RBI double down the left-field line to give Boston the lead, and two batters later, Jacoby Ellsbury ripped an RBI single to bring the lead to 3-1, which would stand up for the victory.

Through Game 5, the Red Sox had won all three World Series contests in which Ross started behind the plate, putting them on the brink of a possible magical clinch at home and third championship ring in the past 10 years. "The fact is, we're going home," said Manager John Farrell. "Going back to a place that our guys love to play in, in front of our fans."

	1	2	3	4	5	6	7	8	9	R	H	E
BOSTON	1	0	0	0	0	0	2	0	0	3	9	0
ST. LOUIS	0	0	0	1	0	0	0	0	0	1	4	0

WP: Lester **LP:** Wainwright **SV:** Uehara
HR: STL: Holliday

Koji Uehara earned his second save of the World Series, striking out Matt Adams in the eighth and retiring the side in the ninth to put Boston up, 3-2.

GAME 5, OCT. 28
RED SOX 3, CARDINALS 1

"THE ONE THING THAT WE'VE SEEN REPEATEDLY THROUGHOUT THE YEAR IS THAT THE AWARE-NESS INSIDE THE GAME, THE WILL TO SUCCEED, AND THE DESIRE TO COMPETE HAVE BEEN PRESENT WITH THIS TEAM FROM DAY ONE."
John Farrell

Clockwise from bottom left: Ross, who hit the go-ahead, RBI double, was thrown out at the plate to end the seventh inning, but not before Ellsbury plated an insurance run with his RBI single. In the fourth, after Holliday sent a moonshot to center and Carlos Beltran nearly went back-to-back, Sox shortstop Drew flashed some impressive leather, leaping to snag a Yadier Molina liner to get Boston out of the inning.

The Cardinals sent ace Wainwright (above) to the mound in Game 5, but he fell short once again — despite striking out 10 batters — allowing three runs on eight hits over seven innings. Holliday put the Redbirds on the board in the fourth with a solo blast to center field.

ACES, ANYTHING BUT WILD

THE BILLING FOR Game 1 of the 2013 World Series listed Jon Lester and Adam Wainwright, two strong arms competing to stifle a set of powerhouse lineups. The result was an 8-1 affair that was anything but a pitchers' duel. But with the Series knotted after Game 4, the aces were set to match up a second time.

For the Red Sox, Lester — who went 7.2 innings with eight K's the first time out — could only hope for a repeat performance. And that was exactly what he delivered, lasting another 7.2 frames — matching a career post-season high — and allowing just one run on a homer to Matt Holliday, while fanning seven and limiting the potent Cards to four hits.

"Watching the way he pitched everybody, he was executing pitches and living in the bottom of the strike zone," said Carlos Beltran, who tallied one of the Cardinals' Game 5 knocks and nearly stroked a homer.

The win was Lester's third in as many starts in World Series play, and gave the Sox an advantage as they headed back home. But there was much to be said about his counterpart, as well. Wainwright also lasted seven frames and made several of those look easy, recording his first six outs against the Sox on K's before leaving the game with a grand total of 10.

Thanks to each starter's efforts at stifling bats, Game 5 ended in just 2 hours and 52 minutes — quite a quick pace for an October matchup.

GAME 6, OCT. 30
RED SOX 6, CARDINALS 1

IT WAS A LONG TIME COMING, TO SAY THE LEAST.

Fenway Park has seen more than its share of memorable moments in its 101-year history, and even quite a few within the last decade, but a night like this was a first in nearly a century. From 1919–2012, six Red Sox teams had reached the World Series, and two had won, but none clinched at their beloved ballpark. In fact, this year was the first time since 1975 that Fenway even hosted a Game 6.

Both the Cardinals and the Sox had a chance to jump ahead early, stranding a total of five base runners through two innings. But Boston's bats finally came alive in the home half of the third, as Jacoby Ellsbury led off the frame with a single, Series MVP David Ortiz was intentionally walked, and Jonny Gomes was hit by a pitch. With two outs, Shane Victorino, already a world champion with the 2008 Phillies, electrified the crowd, drilling a bases-clearing double off the Green Monster to put the home team up, 3-0.

"Fortunately he came up with the bases loaded in two key spots," said Manager John Farrell. "He's had such an uncanny ability to step in in those huge moments — a grand slam against Detroit, a three-run hit tonight."

Starter John Lackey likely experienced some déjà vu as he quieted the Cardinals, thinking back to the time when he won the Game 7 clincher for the 2002 Angels. With this victory, the 35-year-old right-hander became the *only* pitcher to start and win the clinching game of a World Series with two different teams. Although the third-inning run support was all Lackey would need, the Sox kept on pounding Cardinals starter Michael Wacha to tag him for three more runs in the fourth. An unlikely power source, shortstop Stephen Drew kept the scoring going with a solo homer, while Ellsbury and Ortiz came around to score on a pair of walks and three hits.

The insurance runs guaranteed that closer Koji Uehara would be on the mound for the Red Sox's celebration. The Japanese import induced two fly ball outs to left before whiffing Matt Carpenter and leaping into the arms of catcher David Ross as the stadium chanted his name. Good times, indeed, never felt so good.

	1	2	3	4	5	6	7	8	9	R	H	E
ST. LOUIS	0	0	0	0	0	0	1	0	0	1	9	1
BOSTON	0	0	3	3	0	0	0	0	x	6	8	1

WP: Lackey LP: Wacha
HR: BOS: Drew

Red Sox players lined up to watch the Dropkick Murphys, as the Boston-based rock group performed the national anthem.

Lackey turned his stellar postseason into one that made history, becoming the first pitcher to start and win a World Series clincher for two different teams.

GAME 6, OCT. 30
RED SOX 6, CARDINALS 1

"WHEN [TEAMS] GOT TIRED IN SEPTEMBER, WE SEEMED TO GET STRONGER. IT'S A TESTAMENT TO THEIR WILL — THIS CLUB IS STRONG."
John Henry

Victorino (top) notched another clutch postseason hit with a bases-loaded, three-run double off the Monster, giving Boston an early lead. Xander Bogaerts and Ortiz mimicked home plate umpire Jim Joyce's "safe" call as Gomes came around to score the Red Sox's third run.

Wacha earned a Game 2 win by allowing two runs on three hits, but exited Game 6 after just 3.2 innings, on the hook for all six Red Sox runs.

GAME 6, OCT. 30
RED SOX 6, CARDINALS 1

Clockwise from top left: Lackey saluted the raucous Fenway crowd as he exited after tossing 6.2 innings of one-run ball; Drew got it done in Game 6 in the field and at the plate, adding a key insurance run with a solo homer in the fourth; right-handed set-up man Junichi Tazawa performed admirably all postseason, adding to his impressive ledger by setting down Allen Craig after inheriting a bases-loaded, two-out situation in the seventh; Gomes provided a steady glove in left field, recording the first two outs of the ninth inning.

DESIGNATED LEGEND

FANS GREW RESTLESS, but no one could blame the Cardinals for walking David Ortiz four times in Game 6. The problem for the Redbirds, though, was that his damage in the Series had already been done. Big Papi batted .688 in the Fall Classic with six RBI, posting an obscene .750 on-base percentage and giving Cards Manager Mike Matheny no choice but to pitch around him. "These guys have one of the best pitching staffs I've ever faced," Ortiz said. "My key has been to hit only strikes."

In addition to the lethal swing and patience to take a free pass when the situation called for it, Ortiz continued to lead the Red Sox with a smile as big as his bat en route to Fall Classic MVP honors. But he refused to give himself too much credit. "We are not here because of David Ortiz," he said. "We're here because we are a team."

Ortiz raised his lifetime World Series average to .454, which ranks first all time for hitters with more than 50 plate appearances. "We're talking about a Hall-of-Fame-caliber player doing some incredible hitting on this stage," said Manager John Farrell.

As if his hitting exploits weren't enough, Ortiz provided the seminal moment in the Fall Classic when he gathered his teammates for an impromptu pep rally in the dugout prior to the sixth inning of Game 4, when the Red Sox were trailing in the Series, 2 games to 1. At the time, the score was tied 1-1, and Red Sox players not named Ortiz were hitless. "I've given speeches before, but just not on camera," Ortiz said of his motivation. "I saw some guys with their faces down and I thought it was time."

The club responded, as Jonny Gomes launched a three-run homer to put the Red Sox ahead, 4-1, and they wouldn't trail again. "I told my teammates, 'If you think you are always going to come to the World Series, you're wrong, especially playing in the AL East. Do you know how many people we beat up to get to this level? A lot of good teams, and that doesn't happen every year. It took me six years to get back to this stage, and we've had better teams than what we have right now, and we never made it. So take advantage of being here."

Ortiz certainly took advantage of his time on baseball's biggest stage. At one point, he reached base in a record-tying nine consecutive plate appearances. Overall, he got on base three times in five straight games. He proved to be virtually unstoppable, but he focused attention back to the team as a whole.

"I knew it was going to be a special year very early," the three-time champion said. "When we started rolling, nobody was going to stop the train."

> ## "THIS CHAMPIONSHIP IS FOR YOU, BOSTON. YOU'VE BEEN THROUGH A LOT, AND THIS IS FOR YOU. THIS IS OUR *BLEEEEEEP* CITY!"
> David Ortiz

GAME 6, OCT. 30
RED SOX 6, CARDINALS 1

POSTSEASON STATS

NO.	PLAYER	W	L	ERA	SO	BB	SV
PITCHERS							
32	Craig Breslow	1	0	2.45	6	7	0
11	Clay Buchholz	0	0	4.35	17	8	0
46	Ryan Dempster	0	0	3.00	3	0	0
22	Felix Doubront	1	0	1.29	4	3	0
41	John Lackey	3	1	2.77	25	6	0
31	Jon Lester	4	1	1.56	29	8	0
56	Franklin Morales	0	0	6.75	0	2	0
44	Jake Peavy	0	1	7.11	8	4	0
36	Junichi Tazawa	1	0	1.23	6	1	0
19	Koji Uehara	1	1	0.66	16	0	7
67	Brandon Workman	0	1	0.00	4	3	0

NO.	PLAYER	AB	H	AVG	HR	RBI	OBP
CATCHERS							
3	David Ross	25	6	.240	0	2	.269
39	Jarrod Saltalamacchia	32	6	.188	0	5	.257
INFIELDERS							
72	Xander Bogaerts	27	8	.296	0	2	.412
7	Stephen Drew	54	6	.111	1	4	.140
16	Will Middlebrooks	25	4	.160	0	1	.250
12	Mike Napoli	46	10	.217	2	7	.308
34	David Ortiz	51	18	.353	5	13	.500
15	Dustin Pedroia	63	15	.238	0	7	.286
OUTFIELDERS							
50	Quintin Berry	0	0	.000	0	0	.000
37	Mike Carp	8	0	.000	0	1	.000
2	Jacoby Ellsbury	64	22	.344	0	6	.408
5	Jonny Gomes	42	7	.167	1	5	.271
29	Daniel Nava	25	5	.200	0	2	.286
18	Shane Victorino	51	11	.216	1	12	.333

GAME 6, OCT. 30
RED SOX 6, CARDINALS 1

Uehara and Ortiz, the respective ALCS and World Series MVPs, enjoyed a moment of euphoria after clinching Boston's third title in 10 seasons.

"[THE FANS] DESERVEDLY SHARE IN IT. EVERYTHING WE'VE GONE THROUGH IN THIS CITY THIS YEAR, IT'S FITTING THAT THEY'RE HERE TO WITNESS IT. MAYBE THEY DON'T HAVE TO GO 95 YEARS AGAIN TO SEE IT DONE ON OUR HOME FIELD." John Farrell

POSTSEASON HISTORY

Playing in its first Fall Classic under the Red Sox moniker in 1912, Boston edged the New York Giants in a thrilling eight-game series (Game 2 ended in a 6-6 tie and was replayed due to darkness). A misplayed ball by Giants center fielder Fred Snodgrass sparked Boston's series-clinching two-run rally.

1903*
WORLD SERIES

THE BOSTON AMERICANS and the Pittsburgh Pirates met in the inaugural World Series in 1903 in a best-of-nine format to determine the champion. In a Series that featured four future Hall of Famers (Jimmy Collins, Fred Clarke, Cy Young and Honus Wagner), Boston took the title in eight games and second-year outfielder Patsy Dougherty etched his name into the record books; in Game 2, he became the first player to record a multi-homer Fall Classic game. (The day before, the Pirates' Jimmy Sebring hit the first-ever Series longball off Young.)

Dougherty led the AL with 107 runs and 195 hits during the regular season, and had two triples, three runs scored and five RBI in the Series as Boston's leadoff man. Right-hander Deacon Phillippe threw five complete games for

the Pirates, but was out-pitched by Young in Game 7 and would take the loss again in Game 8. Young, the game's great mound star at 36 years old, capped a season in which he won 28-plus games for the third straight year with the only World Series title of his storied 22-year career.

AMERICANS 5, PITTSBURGH PIRATES 3
Oct. 1 Pirates 7 at Americans 3
Oct. 2 Pirates 0 at Americans 3
Oct. 3 Pirates 4 at Americans 2
Oct. 6 Americans 4 at Pirates 5
Oct. 7 Americans 11 at Pirates 2
Oct. 8 Americans 6 at Pirates 3
Oct. 10 Americans 7 at Pirates 3
Oct. 13 Pirates 0 at Americans 3

*Denotes Championship Season

1912*
WORLD SERIES

THE 1912 FALL Classic between the Red Sox and New York Giants was hotly contested over not just seven games, but eight. After the first two games — in which the Red Sox outscored the Giants 10-9 before Game 2 was called due to darkness with the score knotted at six — Rube Marquard took the mound for New York and dominated Boston in a 2-1, Game 3 victory. Boston bounced right back behind ace Smoky Joe Wood, who held the Giants to a lone run in Game 4. Boston took the next game to lead the Series, 3 games to 1, but Marquard got his second complete-game win in Game 6. An 11-4 Game 7 drubbing by the Giants led to a Game 8 at Fenway Park.

In the bottom of the 10th, with the Giants up, 2-1, center fielder Fred Snodgrass dropped a routine fly ball, allowing the batter, Clyde Engle, to reach second. The miscue, which became known as "Snodgrass's Muff," ignited a Red Sox rally that gave them a 3-2, title-sealing win.

RED SOX 4, NEW YORK GIANTS 3
Oct. 8 Red Sox 4 at Giants 3
Oct. 9 Giants 6 at Red Sox 6 (11 innings)
Oct. 10 Giants 2 at Red Sox 1
Oct. 11 Red Sox 3 at Giants 1
Oct. 12 Giants 1 at Red Sox 2
Oct. 14 Red Sox 2 at Giants 5
Oct. 15 Giants 11 at Red Sox 4
Oct. 16 Giants 2 at Red Sox 3 (10 innings)

1915*
WORLD SERIES

THREE YEARS AFTER being pitted against a fellow heavyweight in the Giants, the Red Sox squared off with an underdog Phillies team that emerged from a weak NL crop with 90 wins during the regular season. But stunningly, Ernie Shore lost Game 1 to Grover Cleveland Alexander, 3-1 — though it proved to be just a brief scare.

Boston won the next three games by identical scores of 2-1, and then took the finale 5-4. Left fielder Duffy Lewis hit .444, and Harry Hooper also starred for the Sox, hitting .350. Game 2 featured a historic moment, as Woodrow Wilson became the first President to attend a Fall Classic.

RED SOX 4, PHILADELPHIA PHILLIES 1
Oct. 8 Red Sox 1 at Phillies 3
Oct. 9 Red Sox 2 at Phillies 1
Oct. 11 Phillies 1 at Red Sox 2
Oct. 12 Phillies 1 at Red Sox 2
Oct. 13 Red Sox 5 at Phillies 4

1916*
WORLD SERIES

BABE RUTH MADE his pitching debut in the 1916 Fall Classic as the Red Sox remained undefeated in World Series play. Ruth was the season and World Series hero, with a 23-12 regular-season record and a 1.75 ERA.

After Ernie Shore pitched Boston to victory in Game 1, Ruth took the hill for Game 2, in which a legendary pitcher's duel — since nicknamed a "double masterpiece" — ensued with Brooklyn Robins starter Sherry Smith. The two starters bulldogged through 13 innings, as each allowed just six hits and one run. In the bottom of the 14th, pinch-hitter Del Gainer delivered the walk-off hit, sealing Boston's 2-1 victory.

Upon Ruth's 14-inning, complete-game masterpiece, the Red Sox went on to repeat as World Series champions, winning by an identical 4-games-to-1 ledger.

RED SOX 4, BROOKLYN ROBINS 1
Oct. 7 Robins 5 at Red Sox 6
Oct. 9 Robins 1 at Red Sox 2 (14 innings)
Oct. 10 Red Sox 3 at Robins 4
Oct. 11 Red Sox 6 at Robins 2
Oct. 12 Robins 1 at Red Sox 4

1918*
WORLD SERIES

IN 1918, BABE Ruth was a 23-year-old pitcher already appearing in his third World Series. Two years earlier, he had helped the Red Sox win their second straight championship with a masterful Game 2 performance in which he blanked the Brooklyn Robins for 13 consecutive innings. This time, he would do even more.

In Game 1, Ruth silenced the crowd with a 1-0 shutout of the Cubs and returned to the mound at Fenway Park four days later and pitched the Red Sox to a 3-games-to-1 lead. In that game, Ruth blanked the Cubs for seven innings — extending his then-record streak of consecutive scoreless innings in World Series play to 29 — until they struck for two runs in the top of the eighth. Boston then scored the go-ahead run in the bottom of the frame to take a 3-2 lead. The Sox would go on to clinch the championship in front of the home crowd.

RED SOX 4, CHICAGO CUBS 2
Sept. 5 Red Sox 1 at Cubs 0
Sept. 6 Red Sox 1 at Cubs 3
Sept. 7 Red Sox 2 at Cubs 1
Sept. 9 Cubs 2 at Red Sox 3
Sept. 10 Cubs 3 at Red Sox 0
Sept. 11 Cubs 1 at Red Sox 2

1946
WORLD SERIES
ST. LOUIS CARDINALS 4, RED SOX 3
Oct. 6 Red Sox 3 at Cardinals 2 (10 innings)
Oct. 7 Red Sox 0 at Cardinals 3
Oct. 9 Cardinals 0 at Red Sox 4
Oct. 10 Cardinals 12 at Red Sox 3
Oct. 11 Cardinals 3 at Red Sox 6
Oct. 13 Red Sox 1 at Cardinals 4
Oct. 15 Red Sox 3 at Cardinals 4

1967
WORLD SERIES
ST. LOUIS CARDINALS 4, RED SOX 3
Oct. 4 Cardinals 2 at Red Sox 1
Oct. 5 Cardinals 0 at Red Sox 5
Oct. 7 Red Sox 2 at Cardinals 5
Oct. 8 Red Sox 0 at Cardinals 6
Oct. 9 Red Sox 3 at Cardinals 1
Oct. 11 Cardinals 4 at Red Sox 8
Oct. 12 Cardinals 7 at Red Sox 2

1975
ALCS
RED SOX 3, OAKLAND ATHLETICS 0
Oct. 4 Athletics 1 at Red Sox 7
Oct. 5 Athletics 3 at Red Sox 6
Oct. 7 Red Sox 5 at Athletics 3

Although the Red Sox lost the 1967 Fall Classic in a dramatic seven games, Carl Yastrzemski posted a spectacular .400/.500/.840 slash line with three homers, five RBI and four walks.

WORLD SERIES
CINCINNATI REDS 4, RED SOX 3
Oct. 11 Reds 0 at Red Sox 6
Oct. 12 Reds 3 at Red Sox 2
Oct. 14 Red Sox 5 at Reds 6 (10 innings)
Oct. 15 Red Sox 5 at Reds 4
Oct. 16 Red Sox 2 at Reds 6
Oct. 21 Reds 6 at Red Sox 7 (12 innings)
Oct. 22 Reds 4 at Red Sox 3

1986
ALCS
RED SOX 4, CALIFORNIA ANGELS 3
Oct. 7 Angels 8 at Red Sox 1
Oct. 8 Angels 2 at Red Sox 9
Oct. 10 Red Sox 3 at Angels 5
Oct. 11 Red Sox 3 at Angels 4 (11 innings)
Oct. 12 Red Sox 7 at Angels 6 (11 innings)
Oct. 14 Angels 4 at Red Sox 10
Oct. 15 Angels 1 at Red Sox 8

WORLD SERIES
NEW YORK METS 4, RED SOX 3

Denotes Championship Season

Oct. 18 Red Sox 1 at Mets 0
Oct. 19 Red Sox 9 at Mets 3
Oct. 21 Mets 7 at Red Sox 1
Oct. 22 Mets 6 at Red Sox 2
Oct. 23 Mets 2 at Red Sox 4
Oct. 25 Red Sox 5 at Mets 6 (10 innings)
Oct. 27 Red Sox 5 at Mets 8

1988
ALCS
OAKLAND ATHLETICS 4, RED SOX 0
Oct. 5 Athletics 2 at Red Sox 1
Oct. 6 Athletics 4 at Red Sox 3
Oct. 8 Red Sox 6 at Athletics 10
Oct. 9 Red Sox 1 at Athletics 4

1990
ALCS
OAKLAND ATHLETICS 4, RED SOX 0
Oct. 6 Athletics 9 at Red Sox 1
Oct. 7 Athletics 4 at Red Sox 1
Oct. 9 Red Sox 1 at Athletics 4
Oct. 10 Red Sox 1 at Athletics 3

1995
ALDS
CLEVELAND INDIANS 3, RED SOX 0
Oct. 3 Red Sox 4 at Indians 5 (13 innings)
Oct. 4 Red Sox 0 at Indians 4
Oct. 6 Indians 8 at Red Sox 2

1998
ALDS
CLEVELAND INDIANS 3, RED SOX 1
Sept. 29 Red Sox 11 at Indians 3
Sept. 30 Red Sox 5 at Indians 9
Oct. 2 Indians 4 at Red Sox 3
Oct. 3 Indians 2 at Red Sox 1

1999
ALDS
RED SOX 3, CLEVELAND INDIANS 2
Oct. 6 Red Sox 2 at Indians 3

Oct. 7 Red Sox 1 at Indians 11
Oct. 9 Indians 3 at Red Sox 9
Oct. 10 Indians 7 at Red Sox 23
Oct. 11 Red Sox 12 at Indians 8

ALCS
NEW YORK YANKEES 4, RED SOX 1
Oct. 13 Red Sox 3 at Yankees 4 (10 innings)
Oct. 14 Red Sox 2 at Yankees 3
Oct. 16 Yankees 1 at Red Sox 13
Oct. 17 Yankees 9 at Red Sox 2
Oct. 18 Yankees 6 at Red Sox 1

2003
ALDS
RED SOX 3, OAKLAND ATHLETICS 2
Oct. 1 Red Sox 4 at Athletics 5 (12 innings)
Oct. 2 Red Sox 1 at Athletics 5
Oct. 4 Athletics 1 at Red Sox 3 (11 innings)
Oct. 5 Athletics 4 at Red Sox 5
Oct. 6 Red Sox 4 at Athletics 3

A 24-year-old Roger Clemens started Games 2 and 6 for Boston in the 1986 World Series, allowing nine hits and four runs in 11.1 innings.

Denotes Championship Season

Ortiz authored two iconic walk-off hits on consecutive nights in Games 4 and 5 of the 2004 ALCS, kick-starting Boston's miraculous comeback.

Already a world champion with the Marlins, Beckett kicked off the 2007 Fall Classic with a sterling seven-inning, one-run performance in Game 1.

ALCS
NEW YORK YANKEES 4, RED SOX 3
Oct. 8 Red Sox 5 at Yankees 2
Oct. 9 Red Sox 2 at Yankees 6
Oct. 11 Yankees 4 at Red Sox 3
Oct. 13 Yankees 2 at Red Sox 3
Oct. 14 Yankees 4 at Red Sox 2
Oct. 15 Red Sox 9 at Yankees 6
Oct. 16 Red Sox 5 at Yankees 6 (11 innings)

2004*
ALDS
RED SOX 3, ANAHEIM ANGELS 0
Oct. 5 Red Sox 9 at Angels 3
Oct. 6 Red Sox 8 at Angels 3
Oct. 8 Angels 6 at Red Sox 8 (10 innings)

ALCS
RED SOX 4, NEW YORK YANKEES 3
Oct. 12 Red Sox 7 at Yankees 10
Oct. 13 Red Sox 1 at Yankees 3
Oct. 16 Yankees 19 at Red Sox 8
Oct. 17 Yankees 4 at Red Sox 6 (12 innings)

Oct. 18 Yankees 4 at Red Sox 5 (14 innings)
Oct. 19 Red Sox 4 at Yankees 2
Oct. 20 Red Sox 10 at Yankees 3

WORLD SERIES
ON THE HEELS of the most dramatic come-from-behind victory ever in a playoff series — after being down 3 games to none in the ALCS, against the archrival Yankees no less — the Red Sox and their fans were riding high. But after going 86 years without a world championship, the "Curse of the Bambino" couldn't be extinguished with an AL pennant. Only a World Series victory would suffice, and with Albert Pujols, Jim Edmonds, Scott Rolen and the 105-win Cardinals on the horizon, it appeared Boston had quite the challenge ahead.

Or maybe not. On fire after four straight victories in the ALCS, the Red Sox stepped on the pedal early in the Fall Classic and never let up, scoring four runs in the bottom of the first inning of Game 1 on the way to an 11-9 victory. In Game 2, Sox pitcher Curt Schilling went six innings and gave up just one run despite pitching with a severely injured ankle that bled through his sock during the outing. Things failed to get better for the Cardinals when they returned to St. Louis for Games 3 and 4, as

Denotes Championship Season

the stellar Boston pitching staff — led by Game 3 starter Pedro Martinez and Game 4 starter Derek Lowe — held the Redbirds to just one run in two games. As the Red Sox celebrated on the mound after the final out, 86 years of misery were erased.

RED SOX 4, ST. LOUIS CARDINALS 0
Oct. 23 Cardinals 9 at Red Sox 11
Oct. 24 Cardinals 2 at Red Sox 6
Oct. 26 Red Sox 4 at Cardinals 1
Oct. 27 Red Sox 3 at Cardinals 0

2005
ALDS
CHICAGO WHITE SOX 3, RED SOX 0
Oct. 4 Red Sox 2 at White Sox 14
Oct. 5 Red Sox 4 at White Sox 5
Oct. 7 White Sox 5 at Red Sox 3

2007*
ALDS
RED SOX 3, LOS ANGELS ANGELS 0
Oct. 3 Angels 0 at Red Sox 4
Oct. 5 Angels 3 at Red Sox 6
Oct. 7 Red Sox 9 at Angels 1

ALCS
RED SOX 4, CLEVELAND INDIANS 3
Oct. 12 Indians 3 at Red Sox 10
Oct. 13 Indians 13 at Red Sox 6 (11 innings)
Oct. 15 Red Sox 2 at Indians 4
Oct. 16 Red Sox 3 at Indians 7
Oct. 18 Red Sox 7 at Indians 1
Oct. 20 Indians 2 at Red Sox 12
Oct. 21 Indians 2 at Red Sox 11

WORLD SERIES
THE CURSE WAS broken, and now the word most associated with the Boston Red Sox was "dynasty." After winning it all in 2004 for the first time in 86 years, Boston returned to the World Series in '07 against the upstart Colorado Rockies. The formidable Sox offense was led by veteran third baseman Mike Lowell, just one of the many sluggers on a team headlined by David Ortiz and Manny Ramirez.

After a Game 1 blowout (the Sox won 13-1), Game 2 was a pitchers' duel between Boston's Curt Schilling and Colorado's Ubaldo Jimenez. Lowell's RBI double in the fifth inning proved to be the difference in the 2-1 Red Sox win. In Game 3 — the first-ever World Series game in Colorado — the Red Sox put on another offensive show, and Lowell's surprise steal of third base in the ninth inning led to his scoring Boston's 10th run, slamming the door shut on the Rockies, who had swept the Phillies and Diamondbacks out of the first two rounds.

Lowell didn't let up in Game 4, hitting a solo home run in the seventh inning to give Boston a 3-0 lead. They won the game, 4-3, sweeping the Fall Classic. Series MVP Lowell finished the four games with a .400 batting average, six runs, a homer and four RBI — not bad for a guy who was almost an afterthought in the Josh Beckett trade in 2005.

RED SOX 4, COLORADO ROCKIES 0
Oct. 24 Rockies 1 at Red Sox 13
Oct. 25 Rockies 1 at Red Sox 2
Oct. 27 Red Sox 10 at Rockies 5
Oct. 28 Red Sox 4 at Rockies 3

2008
ALDS
RED SOX 3, LOS ANGELES ANGELS 1
Oct. 1 Red Sox 4 at Angels 1
Oct. 3 Red Sox 7 at Angels 5
Oct. 5 Angels 5 at Red Sox 4 (12 innings)
Oct. 6 Angels 2 at Red Sox 3

ALCS
TAMPA BAY RAYS 4, RED SOX 3
Oct. 10 Red Sox 2 at Rays 0
Oct. 11 Red Sox 8 at Rays 9 (11 innings)
Oct. 13 Rays 9 at Red Sox 1
Oct. 14 Rays 13 at Red Sox 4
Oct. 16 Rays 7 at Red Sox 8
Oct. 18 Red Sox 4 at Rays 2
Oct. 19 Red Sox 1 at Rays 3

2009
ALDS
LOS ANGELES ANGELS 3, RED SOX 0
Oct. 8 Red Sox 0 at Angels 5
Oct. 9 Red Sox 1 at Angels 4
Oct. 11 Angels 7 at Red Sox 6

Denotes Championship Season

The 2011 Cardinals overcame a 3-games-to-2 Fall Classic deficit when the Series returned to their home turf, pulling out a tense 10-9 win in Game 6 to force a Game 7 at Busch Stadium.

NO PLACE LIKE HOME

IT WASN'T LONG AGO THAT THE SCHEDULE for the World Series was set years in advance, with the American and National Leagues annually alternating home-field advantage as hosts to start and end the Series in Games 1, 2, 6 and 7. But after the 2002 All-Star Game ended in a tie, Commissioner Bud Selig upped the ante by awarding home-field advantage in the World Series to the winner of the Midsummer Classic. The move was quite an incentive, since the team with home-field advantage had won 15 of 17 World Series from 1985–2002, including the eight previous Game 7s.

The All-Star Game has been a more spirited affair ever since, and the results have favored the AL, as the Junior Circuit has won eight of the 11 games under the new system. But because it takes the full seven games for home-field advantage to truly matter in the World Series, the edge has not been a significant factor since the Rangers' Hank Blalock first clinched it for the AL with a game-winning home run in the 2003 All-Star Game. That year, the Yankees held home-field advantage but still lost the Series to the Florida Marlins, who clinched the championship in Game 6 at old Yankee Stadium.

Six years later, the Bronx Bombers reversed that fate in the first year of their new ballpark, returning home to finish off a Fall Classic victory over the Phillies in Game 6. But no team enjoyed hosting the decisive contests more than the 2011 Cardinals, who twice tied Game 6, then won it on a walk-off homer by David Freese in the bottom of the 11th. They sealed their stunning title in front of their home fans the next night.

It's clear that the prospect of home-field advantage has been an incentive for All-Star Game participants, no matter how unlikely a World Series berth might seem at the time. In 2008, Tampa Bay entered the second half with a 55-39 record, just a half-game behind the Red Sox in the AL East. Although the Rays had never won more than 70 games in any of their previous 10 seasons, they harbored realistic hopes of a postseason berth when their then-club-record three All-Star representatives arrived in New York.

And they certainly helped the cause. Third baseman Evan Longoria tied the All-Star Game with a double in the eighth inning, catcher Dioner Navarro reached base twice, and left-hander Scott Kazmir worked a scoreless 15th to get the win. "Longoria, Navi and I talked about it when we were there," Kazmir said before the World Series. "We knew this game really meant something to us because in the long run it would give us an advantage, hopefully, in the World Series. You couldn't ask for anything more, especially the way we played here. So in the back of our heads, we knew how much this game meant to us as a team, as an organization."

Alas, the Rays' All-Star efforts and subsequent Fall Classic home-field advantage mattered little, as the Phillies won Game 1 in Tampa before clinching their first World Series crown in 28 years back at home. Philadelphia closer Brad Lidge, who was tagged with the loss in the All-Star Game after allowing the winning run in the 15th inning, was on the mound to record the final out of the Series.

BASEBALLS

EACH RAWLINGS BASEBALL USED IN RECENT FALL Classics is emblazoned with that year's World Series emblem in gold ink. Many of these specially marked balls are already well traveled by the time Game 1 begins, as each of the four teams involved in League Championship Series play receives 30 dozen (360) official World Series balls in anticipation of a win. The losers of the Championship Series in each league must hand over their supply to the ALCS and NLCS winners at the conclusion of each best-of-seven series.

"You could look at it as adding insult to injury, but nobody perceives it as awkward," said Brian O'Gara, MLB's senior director of special events. "It's handled by the equipment managers, and even though they clearly have a rooting interest, it's all part of the job to ensure we're prepared no matter where we end up for the World Series."

With 1,440 balls available for the event, there are more than enough for in-game action. Some are signed by the participating teams and earmarked for players, teams or the Commissioner's Office.

Fans who catch foul balls have the added thrill of receiving a specially marked keepsake. This isn't always the case for batting practice, however, when teams will often use regular-season balls.

EACH BASEBALL USED IN RECENT FALL CLASSICS IS EMBLAZONED WITH THAT YEAR'S EMBLEM IN GOLD INK. FANS WHO CATCH FOUL BALLS HAVE THE THRILL OF RECEIVING A SPECIALLY MARKED KEEPSAKE.

WORLD SERIES MVP

AS IF BECOMING A WORLD SERIES CHAMPION WAS not a sufficient enough reward, the Series' Most Valuable Players have also typically received a trophy and a Chevrolet, the Official Vehicle of Major League Baseball.

The World Series MVP Award was originally given out by the editors of *Sport* magazine in 1955. These days, a committee of baseball writers and Major League Baseball officials chooses the tournament's Most Valuable Player following each Series. In 2012, they tabbed the Giants' Pablo Sandoval, who posted a 1.654 OPS with eight hits and three homers in San Francisco's victory over Detroit.

Through 2012, pitchers had won the World Series MVP Award 27 times, capturing the honor in 12 of the first 14 years it was given out. Numerous Hall of Famers have won the award, including two-time honorees Sandy Koufax (1963 and '65 with the Los Angeles Dodgers), Bob Gibson (1964 and '67 with the St. Louis Cardinals) and Reggie Jackson. Known as "Mr. October" for his clutch World Series hitting, Jackson is the only player to win the award for two teams, the 1973 Oakland Athletics and the '77 New York Yankees.

Some of the more unsung Most Valuable Players of World Series past include Donn Clendenon of the 1969 New York Mets (.357, three home runs, four RBI), Bucky Dent of the 1978 Yankees (.417, three runs, seven RBI) and David Eckstein of the 2006 Cardinals (.364, three runs, four RBI). A good number of light-hitting catchers have boosted their offensive production during the World Series and subsequently taken home MVP honors. It's a group that includes Dodgers backstop Steve Yeager (.286, two home runs, four RBI), who shared the award with his teammates Pedro Guerrero and Ron Cey in 1981, Baltimore's Rick Dempsey in 1983 (.385, one home run, two RBI) and Toronto's Pat Borders in 1992 (.450, one home run, three RBI).

But some stars have been able to carry their regular-season dominance into the World Series. Players who have won a league MVP Award in the same season as the World Series MVP include Koufax, Baltimore's Frank Robinson, Jackson, Pittsburgh's Willie Stargell (who shared his regular-season National League MVP honor with St. Louis's Keith Hernandez in 1979) and Philadelphia's Mike Schmidt.

Pitchers who have won a Cy Young and World Series Most Valuable Player Award in the same season include Bob Turley of the 1958 Yankees, Whitey Ford of the 1961 Yankees, Koufax in both 1963 and '65, Bret Saberhagen of the 1985 Royals, Orel Hershiser of the 1988 Dodgers, and Randy Johnson, who shared his 2001 Series MVP Award with mound-mate Curt Schilling, when their Diamondbacks emerged over the Yankees in seven emotionally charged games just weeks after the 9/11 terrorist attacks.

Sandoval made history when he launched three home runs in Game 1 of the 2012 World Series. He continued his offensive tear throughout the Series to earn MVP honors.

Each team's grounds crew makes painstaking preparations when the World Series comes to town, as the field must look impeccable to fans in person as well as to TV viewers.

GROUNDSKEEPERS

FOR THE GROUNDSKEEPERS WHO MAINTAIN Major League ballfields, the World Series presents a number of challenges. Among them are late-season weather as well as the hordes of journalists, photographers, MLB officials and VIPs who trample the grass just a few hours before the surface must look flawless for a worldwide television audience and be perfect for play.

David Mellor, the director of groundskeeping for the Boston Red Sox, is well known around the Big Leagues for the elaborate patterns he and his crew create in the Fenway Park grass, ranging from the Red Sox logo, to the uniform numbers of Sox stars like Ted Williams, to the B Strong emblem in the wake of the Boston Marathon tragedy. Still, the top priority is always the safety and play quality of the field. "You never want to harm the grass or affect playability," said Mellor, whose talents were first on a national display during the 2004 World Series. "We rotate patterns so we don't get grains in the grass."

As is standard during the regular season, the grass is cut every day the team is at home during the Fall Classic so the field plays consistently. A light coating of sand is applied periodically to encourage growth. Such diligent maintenance helps the grass retain its lush green color.

One way groundskeepers protect the field is by placing a geotextile covering over foul territory during batting practice. But oftentimes, the damage necessitates a total turf replacement during the offseason.

The process of creating patterns in the grass has been around for years, as the first lawn mower was made in the 1830s in England, and the striped look on lawns was very popular in Victorian times. But intricate patterns were not used much in sports early on. A Big League groundskeeper must be able to hide turf blemishes, though, which is how Mellor developed his patterning system. While working on the Brewers' grounds crew in 1993, he had to get Milwaukee's County Stadium turf back in shape after the outfield was ravaged during a Paul McCartney concert.

Although many people assume that patterns are cut into the grass, they're actually created by using large rollers weighing up to 75 pounds. These rollers are either hand-pushed or affixed to riding mowers to flatten grass. Since grass blades that are bent away from your vantage point catch more light, they appear lighter in color. Those bent toward your vantage point catch less and appear darker in color. By bending grass in opposite directions, a pattern can be created.

After the McCartney concert, Mellor and his colleagues camouflaged the outfield as best as they could with a checkerboard pattern, and diverted attention with an elaborate design on the infield turf. When baseball resumed, broadcasters didn't mention the damage from the concert, only the pattern in the grass. Soon Mellor was getting calls from viewers wondering how they could create such patterns in their own lawns. As a result, patterning became common at professional sports venues, and in 2001 Mellor published a how-to book about creating patterns for sports fields or residential lawns.

These days, an intricate pattern in the grass is expected of any World Series host site. The trend is so widespread that a pattern was even painted in center field on the Tampa Bay Rays' artificial turf in 2008.

"You have one opportunity to make a first impression, especially during the World Series," said Mellor. "You try and achieve safety and playability first, but there's no doubt we all take a lot of pride in our patterns."

PRIMETIME

WITH ITS CUTTING-EDGE GRAPHICS, BROADCAST innovations and familiar on-air team of Joe Buck and Tim McCarver, Fox Sports has become virtually synonymous with the World Series. Not bad for a network that didn't even have a sports division until 1994, and didn't broadcast a baseball game of any sort until 1996.

World Series television broadcasts began in 1947 in just four markets: New York City, Washington, D.C., Philadelphia and Schenectady, N.Y. NBC then presented the first coast-to-coast telecast of the World Series in 1951, with Jim Britt providing play-by-play and Russ Hodges giving commentary. NBC held exclusive rights to the event through 1975, using broadcasters such as Vin Scully, Mel Allen and Curt Gowdy.

From 1976–89, NBC and ABC alternated years of World Series coverage. In 1985, McCarver — himself a World Series veteran — broadcast his first Fall Classic for ABC. The 2013 Classic marked his record-setting 23rd in the booth. "When you're announcing, you're at the mercy of the game," he says. "Broadcasting a World Series game is far tougher than playing in it."

In 1995, the short-lived Baseball Network got in on the action, splitting coverage of the World Series between ABC and NBC. Fox Sports and NBC began to alternate years of Fall Classic coverage in 1996, with Fox taking even years and NBC taking odd. In 2000, Fox signed a six-year agreement with Major League Baseball that included exclusive rights to the World Series through 2006, a deal later extended to include the Fall Classic through 2013.

Preparation for a World Series broadcast begins shortly after the All-Star Game, as producers begin compiling footage and background information on players from teams in contention at the halfway point. Any such stories must be somewhat generic, though, since baseball players are a notoriously superstitious bunch and will not discuss anything postseason-related — let alone the World Series — prematurely.

Aside from rampant superstition, one of the biggest challenges in presenting the World Series is catering to both hardcore fans and those who might be tuning in for the very first time all year. Even the most avid baseball fan might not be that familiar with a team that surges unexpectedly to the top of the pack after a few seasons of anonymity.

"You spend a few innings of the first game bringing people up to speed," said Pete Macheska, the lead producer for Fox's World Series coverage. These days, a World Series broadcast on Fox involves an on-site crew of 125 individuals.

During the regular season, Fox usually uses seven or eight cameras for a Saturday broadcast. But for the Fall Classic, that number balloons to about 40. Some of the more unusual camera placements include one high above center field that can provide a direct shot of home plate, unlike the standard manned camera that tends to be a little off on the ball-strike calls. There are also in-ground cameras in front of home plate and first base, and wireless cameras that allow a cameraman to walk onto the field after home runs and closely follow the batter from third base to home. Tampa Bay's Tropicana Field, one of the last remaining fixed-domed ballparks, provided Fox the opportunity to install cameras in the catwalks. In 2012, as part of its live HD coverage, Fox unveiled a special high-frame rate SloMo camera for an unprecedented view of the action.

With the many camera angles, umpires are scrutinized more than ever before. "Not that long ago, you might have seen two angles on a replay," Macheska said. "Now we can zoom in, do the super slo-mo and see it from every angle."

The technology can contribute to World Series plot lines, even inadvertently. In 2006, a television producer was monitoring Game 2 on a big-screen TV in a production truck when he noticed what appeared to be a foreign substance on the hand of Tigers pitcher Kenny Rogers. It was brought to the attention of Buck and McCarver during a commercial break and immediately discussed on air.

Thus began the pine tar controversy of that year's Fall Classic. The next day, when the Fox producers and on-air team were having their daily 15-minute sit-downs with each of the managers, Detroit's Jim Leyland suggested the network went looking for controversy.

"The perception is that we go looking for that stuff and it's just not the case," Macheska said. "We follow and report on the story. We don't create it."

Buck and McCarver

FENWAY PARK

ATTENDING A GAME AT FENWAY PARK IS MORE THAN a day at the ballpark — it's a life experience. From its elongated shape, to the looming Green Monster, to the colorful vendors who station their carts outside the stadium, everything about Fenway is different. It's baseball history still being lived in real time as it's passed down through generations. This is a place where a boy who worships Dustin Pedroia might attend a game with his dad who idolized Carl Yastrzemski or his grandfather who loved Ted Williams.

Baseball's oldest current stadium opened five days after the Titanic sank in 1912, but it wasn't the gem we know today. When Babe Ruth played his formative years there, the giant wall in left field wasn't yet called the Green Monster. In fact, it wasn't even green. Instead, it was peppered with advertisements for products like Pureoxia Ginger Ale and Mumm's Extra Rye Whiskey. At its base was Duffy's Cliff, a steep incline that seemed to cause problems for every outfielder except the Sox's Duffy Lewis.

The Monster was finally painted green in 1947, seats were added atop it in 2003 and today, thousands of dents later, it still stands proudly as a pockmarked ambassador of the game's storied past.

BIRTH OF THE RED SOX

BOSTON BASEBALL TRACES ITS ROOTS BACK TO THE 1870s. The support Bostonians gave their NL team convinced executive Ban Johnson that the city would be a strong charter entry into his new American League. Originally, the club was called the Boston Americans, beginning play on April 26, 1901. They finished second that year and then won the first World Series in 1903. The Americans played from 1901–07 before changing their name.

The Americans adopted the name Red Sox — chosen by team owner John I. Taylor in lieu of previous Boston teams that had been known as the "Red Stockings" — late in 1907. The name has remained ever since. The franchise put together one of the more dominant teams at the start of the 1900s. The club won the World Series in 1912, '15, '16 and '18, largely behind the efforts of a pitcher and part-time hitter named Babe Ruth.

THE ROSTER

THE 2013 BOSTON RED SOX

JOHN FARRELL
MANAGER

COMING BACK TO Boston was a smart choice for Farrell, who served as the Red Sox's pitching coach from 2007–10. In his first season as manager, the former Big League starting pitcher orchestrated a 28-game turnaround, as the club went an AL-best 97-65 after finishing last in the AL East in 2012, en route to its third World Series in the last 10 years.

COACHING STAFF:
Arnie Beyeler: First Base
Brian Butterfield: Third Base
Greg Colbrunn: Hitting
Dana LeVangie: Bullpen
Torey Lovullo: Bench
Juan Nieves: Pitching

53

ANDREW BAILEY
PITCHER

SERVING AS THE closer for part of the season, Bailey converted six of his first seven save opportunities before going down with a right shoulder injury in July. The former AL Rookie of the Year and two-time All-Star fanned 39 over 28.2 innings, holding lefties to a .185 average.

40

QUINTIN BERRY
OUTFIELD

WHEN BERRY WAS traded to the Red Sox in a deal with the Royals on Aug. 27, the speedster had yet to be caught swiping a bag in his career. Through the ALCS, Berry was a perfect 28 for 28 in stolen base attempts. He made the most of his eight regular-season at-bats, too, notching five hits — including his third career homer — and four RBI.

50

XANDER BOGAERTS
INFIELD

CALLED UP IN late August, Bogaerts — regarded as the Sox's best prospect — hit his first home run against the Yankees on Sept. 7. The 21-year-old later became the youngest player in franchise history to start a playoff game, surpassing Babe Ruth. He recorded three extra-base hits in the ALCS.

72

JACKIE BRADLEY JR.
OUTFIELD

BRADLEY MADE THE Big League club out of Spring Training and was its Opening Day left fielder. He drove in a run in each of his first three games in the Majors and further proved why he was a 2011 first-round draft pick by showcasing his athleticism in the field.

25

CRAIG BRESLOW
PITCHER

THE YALE GRADUATE enjoyed a banner year in his first full season in Boston, posting a career-low 1.81 ERA. He notched a win in the clinching Game 4 of the ALDS — part of the seven scoreless innings he threw in the first two rounds combined during his first career postseason.

32

DRAKE BRITTON
PITCHER

BRITTON MADE HIS Major League debut on July 20 against the Yankees, tossing a scoreless ninth inning. The rookie southpaw went on to start his career with seven scoreless appearances. He finished the season with a 3.86 ERA in 18 games.

66

CLAY BUCHHOLZ
PITCHER

IN THE FIRST half of the season, Buchholz was as lights-out as any Big League pitcher. He went a perfect 6-0 over his first six starts, throwing at least seven innings in all of them and whiffing 10-plus hitters twice. With his former pitching coach John Farrell at the helm, Buchholz regained his form from 2010, a year in which he won 17 games.

Buchholz was the AL Pitcher of the Month in April, and was named to his second All-Star team in July. After being sidelined in the middle of the season with a neck injury, he returned on Sept. 10 and pitched five innings to record his 10th win of the year. The righty finished with a 12-1 record and a career-low 1.74 ERA.

MIKE CARP
OUTFIELD

CARP CAME TO Boston in a trade with Seattle to provide the Red Sox with power off the bench. He hit .300 off right-handed pitching and slugged eight longballs, highlighted by the pinch-hit, go-ahead grand slam he smashed against the Rays on Sept. 11.

37

RYAN DEMPSTER
PITCHER

AS A VETERAN presence on the Red Sox, Dempster provided depth at the back end of the rotation in his 16th season in the Bigs, his first with the Red Sox. The only active pitcher in MLB with 100-plus wins and 60-plus saves, he put together 14 quality starts before joining the bullpen late in the season.

46

FELIX DOUBRONT
PITCHER

DOUBRONT STARTED THE 2013 season by winning three of his first four decisions. The 25-year-old Venezuela native went on to win 11 games for the second straight season, going 6-4 at Fenway Park with a home 3.84 ERA.

22

STEPHEN DREW
SHORTSTOP

ONE OF SEVERAL savvy offseason acquisitions signed to a one-year deal, Drew tied his career-high with 67 RBI, recorded 50 extra-base hits and posted the second-highest OPS (.777) among AL shortstops. He showed patience at the plate, drawing 54 walks, while providing his usual steady defense.

7

JACOBY ELLSBURY
OUTFIELD

BOSTON'S LEADOFF HITTER, Ellsbury returned to form after an injury-plagued 2012 campaign. The Major League leader in stolen bases swiped 50-plus bags for the third time in his career. Ellsbury also tied for seventh in the Bigs with eight triples and second on the Red Sox with 172 hits, while smashing three leadoff homers this season and providing Gold Glove–caliber defense in center field.

His hot hitting stretched into the postseason, in which he went a combined 16 for 40 (.400) with six stolen bases in the first two rounds. Always the club's spark plug, Ellsbury contributed to many of the Sox's tide-turning, late-inning rallies, scoring on both of their monumental grand slams in the ALCS.

JONNY GOMES
OUTFIELD

SIGNED DURING THE offseason to be an outfield platoon option, Gomes became much more. He was one of the first Red Sox players to experiment with his facial hair, kick-starting the Boston beards craze and helping create the chemistry that defined these Red Sox. He was also one of their best hitters with runners in scoring position, batting at a .346 clip, which ranked in the top 10 among Major League outfielders. Gomes hit a leadoff single and scored the walk-off run in the club's unforgettable comeback win in Game 2 of the ALCS.

JOEL HANRAHAN
PITCHER

BOSTON ACQUIRED HANRAHAN in an offseason trade with the Pittsburgh Pirates. The two-time All-Star recorded his 100th career save on May 2 in Toronto with a scoreless ninth inning, before sustaining an elbow injury that required season-ending Tommy John surgery.

52

BROCK HOLT
INFIELD

HOLT SPENT TIME at second and third base with Boston this season after coming over in a trade with the Pirates, who selected him in the ninth round of the 2009 Draft. He drove in 11 runs in 26 games.

26

JOHN LACKEY
PITCHER

AT 34 YEARS OLD, Lackey bounced back from 2011 Tommy John surgery in a big way. He posted his best ERA (3.52) since 2007 and a career-low walk rate (1.9 BB/9 across 189.1 innings) during the regular season, then delivered perhaps the most critical pitching performance of the postseason, outdueling Justin Verlander with 6.2 shutout frames in ALCS Game 3.

41

RYAN LAVARNWAY
CATCHER

LAVARNWAY THRIVED IN limited action this season, hitting .299 with a .758 OPS in 25 games. The backup catcher contributed to one of the more memorable games of the regular season, slugging the fifth home run of his career during the Red Sox's 20-4 onslaught against the Tigers on Sept. 4.

20

JON LESTER
PITCHER

LESTER STARTED STRONG in his eighth season in Boston, winning his first six decisions while posting a 2.72 ERA. An extended All-Star break — Manager John Farrell chose to push his first second-half start back to give him a breather — ensured that he finished strong, too. The lefty was in peak form in the second half, going 7-2 with a 2.57 ERA to seal his fifth 15-win season. He kept it up in the postseason, posting a 2.33 ERA in the first two rounds.

31

WILL MIDDLEBROOKS
THIRD BASE

IN HIS SECOND season, Middlebrooks turned a corner during the second half, posting the fifth-best OPS (.805) among AL third basemen after the All-Star break. He finished with 17 homers in just 94 games after slugging 15 in 75 contests as a rookie. Three of those longballs came on April 7, when he became the 26th player in franchise history — and just the third third baseman — to hit three homers in one game.

16

ANDREW MILLER
PITCHER

MILLER ENJOYED A career year before a foot injury ended his season in July. The former top starting pitching prospect has turned into a dominant lefty reliever, striking out a whopping 14.1 per nine innings in 2013 while posting a 2.64 ERA.

30

FRANKLIN MORALES
PITCHER

THE VENEZUELA NATIVE continued to shut down lefties in 2013, holding them to a .184 average with no extra-base hits in 38 at-bats. Morales shined as an additional southpaw out of the bullpen during the second half, allowing just three runs in 13 innings pitched.

56

MIKE NAPOLI
FIRST BASE

THE RED SOX found themselves one of the best bargains of the offseason when they signed Napoli to a one-year, $13-million deal. While the 32-year-old's power came as no surprise — he slugged 20-plus homers for the sixth straight year — his quick transition from catcher to Gold Glove–quality first baseman, with an MLB-high 9.7 Ultimate Zone Rating, made him a two-way force. On top of that, he immediately bought into the team's free-wheeling, beard-growing culture and hit two huge home runs in the ALCS, accounting for the lone run off Justin Verlander in the 1-0 Game 3 win.

12

DANIEL NAVA
OUTFIELD

NAVA ENTERED 2013 as a platoon outfielder and turned into one of the season's most pleasant surprises. He posted career highs across the board and embodied the Red Sox's patient approach at the plate, finishing second on the team in on-base percentage (.385) and third in pitches per plate appearance (4.11). No contribution he made outweighed the lift he gave Boston on April 20 — the day the Sox returned to Fenway Park for the first time since the marathon bombing — when he hit the go-ahead three-run homer in the eighth inning of a 4-3 victory.

29

DAVID ORTIZ
DESIGNATED HITTER

AS IF "BIG PAPI" could become any more beloved in Boston, 2013 happened. Not only did he put together the seventh 30-plus-homer, 100-plus-RBI campaign of his career, but he also emerged as an ambassador for the city after tragedy struck in the season's first month. Ortiz lifted spirits with his instantly famous words — "This is our [expletive] city!" — when the Red Sox returned to Fenway Park, and did the same with his bat six months later.

With the club four outs away from heading to Detroit in a 2-games-to-none ALCS hole, its clutch cleanup man came through with another signature October moment, sending the first pitch from Tigers closer Joaquin Benoit over the right-field wall for a game-tying grand slam. The blast proved to be the turning point in both the series and Boston's dream post-season run.

34

JAKE PEAVY
PITCHER

WITH THE ADDITION of a second Wild Card spot in each league in 2012, teams have become increasingly wary about selling at the trade deadline, clinging to the hopes of sneaking into the postseason with their current core intact. The lowly White Sox, however, were willing to ship veteran righty Peavy to Boston on July 30 as part of a three-team deal that also sent Red Sox shortstop Jose Iglesias to Detroit. Peavy immediately plugged a hole in an ailing rotation, going 4-1 with a 4.04 ERA in 10 starts after the trade. Even after Clay Buchholz returned from the DL, Peavy retained his spot in the rotation through the postseason. The former NL Cy Young winner pitched 5.2 innings of one-run ball in Game 4 of the ALDS, pushing the Sox past the Rays for a spot in the ALCS.

DUSTIN PEDROIA
SECOND BASE

IN THIS GOLDEN Age of Boston sports, few players are as associated with grit and victory as Pedroia. A fiery rookie on the 2007 world champion team, the diminutive second baseman has aged gracefully into his role as team leader, bringing his squad to the promised land once more. The former Rookie of the Year and MVP was elected to his fourth All-Star Game in 2013, and finished the year batting .301 with nine homers, 84 RBI, 17 stolen bases and 73 walks. Pedroia made his veteran presence felt, playing in 160 games and stepping up to the plate an AL-leading 724 times. And after signing a seven-year, $100- million contract extension in July, many more Fenway Park plate appearances are sure to follow.

DAVID ROSS
CATCHER

BEHIND ROSS'S MASK is a beard a bit more gray than his younger team-mates'. But the 36-year-old backup catcher filled in admirably behind the plate. Signed in the offseason after 11 years with several National League teams, Ross provided some pop off the bench, hitting four homers and 10 RBI in 102 at-bats. His veteran presence earned him a spot on the postseason roster, where, thanks to the rapport he had quickly established with veteran pitchers Jon Lester and John Lackey, he earned starts in each round of the postseason.

JARROD SALTALAMACCHIA
CATCHER

IN HIS THIRD full year in Boston, Saltalamacchia enjoyed his best offensive season to date. The Red Sox catcher batted a personal-best .273, hitting 14 homers and driving in 65 runs (another career mark), while playing in 121 games, matching his total from a year ago. Salty's OBP (.338), slugging percentage (.466) and OPS (.804) were also career-bests.

39

JUNICHI TAZAWA
PITCHER

COMING OFF A sparkling 2012 campaign in which he posted a 1.43 ERA in 44.0 innings, Tazawa saw an increased workload in 2013, and rose to the challenge. The Japan native became an eighth-inning staple in front of Koji Uehara, recording 25 holds while striking out more than one batter per inning (9.5 K/9).

36

KOJI UEHARA
PITCHER

IT TOOK A few months for the pieces to fall into place for Uehara, but once they did, his results were unparalleled. The 38-year-old journeyman reliever assumed the closer's role once Joel Hanrahan and Andrew Bailey went down with season-ending injuries and put on one of the most dominant relief pitching performances ever. Uehara saved 21 games in 24 opportunities, posting an MLB-record 0.57 WHIP (min. 50 IP). Late in the season, the Red Sox closer strung together two incomprehensible streaks, holding opponents scoreless for 30.1 consecutive innings and retiring 37 batters in a row — the equivalent of roughly one-and-a-third perfect games.

19

SHANE VICTORINO
OUTFIELD

ALTHOUGH MANY LOOKED at the contract the Red Sox handed Victorino before the season as a gamble, he came to Boston with a championship pedigree and something to prove, and played like it in 2013. The 10-year veteran outfielder hit a career-high .294, contributing 15 home runs, 61 RBI and 21 stolen bases from the No. 2 spot in the lineup. Two years removed from his last of five consecutive postseason appearances with the Phillies, Victorino announced his emphatic return to baseball's grandest stage with a go-ahead grand slam in Game 6 of the ALCS, propelling the Red Sox to clinch the AL pennant.

18

ALLEN WEBSTER
PITCHER

A VALUABLE PIECE in Boston's midsummer blockbuster trade with Los Angeles in 2012, Webster split time between Triple-A Pawtucket and the Majors in 2013, making several crucial spot starts for Boston throughout the season. The rookie righty earned his first Big League win on Independence Day, allowing just two runs in six innings against the Padres.

64

ALEX WILSON
PITCHER

TAKEN BY THE Red Sox in the second round of the 2009 Draft, Wilson made his Major League debut this season, providing solid pitching out of the bullpen. The righty reliever logged his first 27.2 Big League innings, holding lefties to a .200 average, with just four extra-base hits allowed in 67 batters faced.

63

BRANDON WORKMAN
PITCHER

WORKMAN MADE A solid Major League debut for the Red Sox, showing his versatility as both a starter and reliever. After beginning the season in Double-A, the right-hander was swiftly promoted to Triple-A and eventually to the Majors in early July. In 20 appearances — including three starts — Workman finished 6-3, striking out more than one batter per inning (10.2 K/9). He pitched his way onto the postseason roster and showed up in a big way in his first playoff appearances, going 5.1 combined innings in the first two rounds, allowing four hits and no runs.

67

2013 SEASON IN REVIEW

IT'S OFTEN SAID THAT PLAYING THE GAME of baseball requires a short memory — an ability to quickly move on from past failures and refocus on future success.

In 2013, some teams embraced the clean slate the new season offered, vanquishing ghosts that had lingered from a couple of months to a couple of decades. The Red Sox spit out the bitter taste of 2012 and replaced it with champagne following the American League's best regular-season run. The Dodgers and Pirates each put losing records in their rear-view mirrors — L.A. 11 weeks of struggles, Pittsburgh 20 years — to turn the summer months into a high-speed thrill ride.

But still, other headliners proved that history has a way of repeating itself. Cincinnati's Homer Bailey experienced deja vu in July, authoring 2013's first no-hitter 277 days after completing 2012's last, while Ichiro Suzuki stroked a base hit in August — something he'd done 3,999 times before, only this time with more meaning.

When the dust from thousands of slides home cleared, it all added up to a year defined by one word: unforgettable.

BEST OF 2013

RULE OF THREES

Some say that bad things come in threes. Three times this year, a pitcher lost a no-hitter with two outs in the ninth inning. It started on April 2 with the Rangers' Yu Darvish, and happened again on Sept. 6 with the Giants' Yusmeiro Petit. Then, Cardinals rookie **Michael Wacha** fell short on Sept. 24.

But good things come in threes, too. Homer Bailey threw the season's first no-hitter on July 2, followed by Tim Lincecum on July 13. On Sept. 29, the regular season's final day, Henderson Alvarez completed 2013's third no-no, balancing out the near-misses.

FINAL STANDINGS

AMERICAN LEAGUE

East	W	L	GB
xBoston	97	65	–
yTampa Bay	92	71	5.5
Baltimore	85	77	12
New York	85	77	12
Toronto	74	88	23

Central	W	L	GB
xDetroit	93	69	–
yCleveland	92	70	1
Kansas City	86	76	7
Minnesota	66	96	27
Chicago	63	99	30

West	W	L	GB
xOakland	96	66	–
Texas	91	72	5.5
Los Angeles	78	84	18
Seattle	71	91	25
Houston	51	111	45

NATIONAL LEAGUE

East	W	L	GB
xAtlanta	96	66	–
Washington	86	76	10
New York	74	88	22
Philadelphia	73	89	23
Miami	62	100	34

Central	W	L	GB
xSt. Louis	97	65	–
yPittsburgh	94	68	3
yCincinnati	90	72	7
Milwaukee	74	88	23
Chicago	66	96	31

West	W	L	GB
xLos Angeles	92	70	–
Arizona	81	81	11
San Diego	76	86	16
San Francisco	76	86	16
Colorado	74	88	18

x Division winner; y Wild Card

2013 CATEGORY LEADERS

AMERICAN LEAGUE

Batting Average	Miguel Cabrera, Detroit	.348
Hits	Adrian Beltre, Texas	199
Home Runs	Chris Davis, Baltimore	53
RBI	Chris Davis, Baltimore	138
Stolen Bases	Jacoby Ellsbury, Boston	52
Wins	Max Scherzer, Detroit	21
ERA	Anibal Sanchez, Detroit	2.57
Strikeouts	Yu Darvish, Texas	277
Saves	Jim Johnson, Baltimore	50

NATIONAL LEAGUE

Batting Average	Michael Cuddyer, Colorado	.331
Hits	Matt Carpenter, St. Louis	199
Home Runs	Pedro Alvarez, Pittsburgh	36
	Paul Goldschmidt, Arizona	
RBI	Paul Goldschmidt, Arizona	125
Stolen Bases	Eric Young Jr., New York	46
Wins	Adam Wainwright, St. Louis	19
	Jordan Zimmermann, Wash.	
ERA	Clayton Kershaw, Los Angeles	1.83
Strikeouts	Clayton Kershaw, Los Angeles	232
Saves	Craig Kimbrel, Atlanta	50

MARCH/APRIL 2013

CLEAN SWEEP

The **Dominican Republic** became the first unbeaten team in World Baseball Classic history, going 8-0 and defeating Puerto Rico, 3-0, in the 2013 title game at AT&T Park on March 19.

B STRONG

On April 20, the Red Sox returned to Fenway for the first time since the Boston Marathon bombing. While the nation mourned, David Ortiz urged Boston to stay strong, declaring, "This is our [expletive] city."

ALMOST PERFECT

Yu Darvish pitched 8.2 perfect innings on April 2, his first start of 2013. But with one out left to record, the Astros' Marwin Gonzalez singled through his legs to break up what would have been MLB's 24th perfecto. Darvish went on to reel off 11 more double-digit strikeout games.

FINDING A HOME

Evan Gattis forfeited a scholarship to Texas A&M and spent four years doing odd jobs before returning to baseball. In his MLB debut on April 3, he showed that he finally found his calling, going deep against Roy Halladay in his second at-bat. Before long, Atlanta had gotten off to a sizzling 12-1 start, and Gattis was April's NL Rookie of the Month for his six home runs and .566 slugging percentage. Meanwhile, the Upton brothers hit back-to-back homers on April 23 and veteran starter Tim Hudson earned his 200th win on April 30.

AFTER FINISHING 69-93 in 2012, last in the AL East, not much was expected of the Red Sox on Opening Day. But from the get-go, new Manager John Farrell and his hodge-podge roster set a winning tone in Boston, letting Red Sox fans know that this season would not be like the last.

Veteran ace **Jon Lester** took the hill on April 1 and opened the campaign with a seven-strikeout performance against the Yankees in the Bronx, kicking off a solid April in which he finished 4-0 with a 3.11 ERA. Boston received sterling moundwork from Clay Buchholz, as well. The seventh-year righty also went undefeated in the first month of the season at 5-0 with a microscopic 1.19 ERA, pitching at least seven innings in all five starts.

While the Red Sox rolled — their 18-8 April record was the best mark in MLB — the city of Boston endured a terrible tragedy in the April 15 Boston Marathon bombings. Through their spirited play on the field and community outreach, the Red Sox did what they could to uplift a grieving city, including honoring first responders at the first game back at Fenway and throughout the season. In that April 20 contest, outfielder Daniel Nava hit an emotional go-ahead, three-run homer in the eighth inning of a 4-3 Red Sox win.

MAY 2013

THE CYCLIST

Angels phenom **Mike Trout**'s eighth-inning long-ball against the Mariners on May 21 made him the youngest player in AL history — and the first of the season — to hit for the cycle. Trout finished the night 4 for 5 with five RBI. The Astros' Brandon Barnes and Rangers' Alex Rios joined him in completing the cycle later this season.

MANNY HITS

Orioles phenom **Manny Machado** went 2 for 3 against the Nationals on May 30 for his 41st multi-hit game, passing Ty Cobb for the most multi-hit outings in MLB history before turning 21. Machado's success, and the rise of power hitter Chris Davis, made the Orioles one of the year's must-see teams, as they boasted five All-Stars and ranked in the top five in runs, doubles, home runs, total bases, RBI and slugging percentage.

SIX FOR SEGURA

On May 28, **Jean Segura** became the first player in four years to record six hits in a game, going 6 for 7 in an extra-inning loss to the Twins. The Brewers standout made the NL All-Star team in his first full Major League season.

AS NEW ACQUISITIONS WERE proving their worth to Red Sox Nation, top-of-the-order mainstay **Jacoby Ellsbury** had to worry about no such thing. Despite missing time in an injury-plagued 2012, it didn't take all that long for the center fielder to vault himself back among the good graces of the Boston faithful.

Trailing, 5-2, against Cleveland on May 26, the Red Sox rallied for four runs in the bottom of the ninth inning to win in walk-off fashion — one of their 11 walk-offs in 2013 — courtesy of Ellsbury's two-run double to center. The rest of his season was a true return to form, including a Major League–leading 52 stolen bases, the third time in his career he reached the half-century mark.

Late-inning heroics were infectious among Red Sox hitters, as shortstop Stephen Drew knocked a walk-off, 11th-inning double against the Twins on May 6, securing a 6-5 victory after the Red Sox blew a 5-4 lead in the ninth. Second-year third baseman Will Middlebrooks also contributed, hitting a three-run double in the top of the ninth on May 16 in Tampa, turning a 3-1 deficit into a 4-3 lead that would hold up.

A day later, righty reliever Koji Uehara pitched a spotless 10th inning in Minnesota, wrapping up a 3-2 victory and earning his first save of the year. Although the closer's role wasn't firmly in Uehara's hands at that point, his cool performance under pressure was a sign of things to come.

JUNE 2013

DRAFT-DAY DRAMA

The Astros made Stanford University pitcher **Mark Appel** the 2013 Draft's first pick on June 6, kicking off a weekend of amazing stories. Brothers D.J. and Dustin Peterson were both taken in the top 50, and Arizona ceremoniously selected paralyzed outfielder Cory Hahn in the 34th round.

STEERING THE SHIP

Gerrit Cole, the No. 1 pick of the 2011 Draft, made his MLB debut with the Pirates on June 11, and won his first four starts. Pittsburgh remained consistent throughout 2013 thanks to its stellar pitching staff (3.26 ERA, third-best in the Majors), with Cole winning 10 games and striking out 100 in 117.1 innings.

QUICK WORK

On June 3, the Dodgers called up Cuban outfielder **Yasiel Puig**, who instantly became the talk of MLB. In 26 June games, Puig posted 44 hits and a .436 average — the highest ever for a rookie in his first month. He helped the Dodgers go from worst to first in the NL West.

AT 37 YEARS OLD and on the heels of an injury-shortened season, it appeared **David Ortiz**'s days as a Major League star were numbered. Of course, nobody relayed this memo to Big Papi, who continued to rake from the middle of the Red Sox's lineup.

Further creeping up on former Seattle Mariner Edgar Martinez for the title of Greatest Designated Hitter Ever, Ortiz powered the Red Sox offense with a team-leading seven homers and 22 RBI in June. Both totals were single-month season highs for Papi, who tallied 30-plus homers and 100-plus RBI (30, 103) for the seventh time in his career, accompanying a .309 batting average.

In the shadow of the Green Monster, a two-headed beast reared its head in first-year Red Sox platoon partners Mike Carp and Jonny Gomes. The left fielders played in 16 and 15 June games, respectively, but it didn't seem to matter which one was in the lineup, as offensive production was bountiful from both bats. Carp boasted a .367/.448/.735 slash line while racking up five home runs and 12 RBI; Gomes batted .304, with six of his 14 hits going for extra bases.

The Red Sox went 17-11 for the month, and were 50-34 overall — 2.5 games ahead of Baltimore for first place in the division — when June was all said and done.

JULY 2013

NO HITS, ALL HOMER

After capping an eventful 2012 campaign with a Sept. 28 no-no, Reds righty **Homer Bailey** threw the first no-hitter of 2013 on July 2 against San Francisco. Not to be outdone, Giants starter Tim Lincecum threw a no-no of his own less than two weeks later (July 13) against the San Diego Padres.

BIG APPLE, BIG STARS

While Miguel Cabrera and Chris Davis put on historic power displays in the first half to earn starting nods in the Midsummer Classic on July 16, the All-Star Game itself was all about **Mariano Rivera**, who received a standing ovation, pitched a perfect eighth and won the game's MVP Award.

SHOWSTOPPER

Oakland A's slugger **Yoenis Cespedes** beat Washington's Bryce Harper, 9-8, in the Home Run Derby finals — held on July 15 at Citi Field — to become the first non–All-Star ever to take home the title. Cespedes hit 17 shots in the first round, more than any other player in the first two rounds combined.

A PERFECT EXAMPLE of the kind of player Boston had in its crosshairs prior to 2013, **Mike Napoli** was a consistent, dependable, relatively inexpensive bat who could contribute in a variety of ways on a day-in, day-out basis.

By July, Napoli had earned his keep — or more specifically, his $13 million. The 2012 All-Star catcher had transformed into an everyday first baseman, and at the halfway point in 2013, he was batting .259 with 11 homers and 58 RBI, the latter two both good for second on the team. In the third game of the second half, he made a statement with an 11th-inning walk-off homer against the Yankees on July 21. The Sox earned a crucial victory off the field just two days later, signing longtime second baseman Dustin Pedroia to a seven-year $100-million extension.

The club capped off the month with a thriller on its last day, winning a 15-inning bout against the Mariners on Stephen Drew's walk-off single. More importantly, the victory helped Boston leap-frog the Rays for first place in the AL East, a spot they would not relinquish for the rest of the season.

AUGUST 2013

GOTCHA

In one of the season's quirkier moments, the Rays' **Evan Longoria** successfully executed the hidden-ball trick on the Dodgers' Juan Uribe, tagging him out when he stepped off third base to speak with coach Tim Wallach during an Aug. 10 contest. The Rockies' Todd Helton fooled the Cardinals' Matt Carpenter with the same fakeout five weeks later.

WORLD HISTORY

Ichiro Suzuki became the sixth professional baseball player ever to reach 4,000 career hits on Aug. 21. He registered 1,278 during his nine seasons in Japan before moving on to MLB's Mariners and Yankees and racking up the next 2,742 in 13 seasons. He joined ranks with Pete Rose, Ty Cobb, Hank Aaron, Stan Musial and Jigger Statz.

ROAD WARRIORS

The **Dodgers** recorded the fourth-longest road winning streak in MLB history, emerging victorious in 15 straight away games before finally losing in St. Louis, 5-1, on Aug. 6. The club had seven come-from-behind wins during the streak, and finished it in first place in the NL West.

WITH CLAY BUCHHOLZ on the disabled list for a considerable chunk of the summer, Boston made a splash for a starting pitcher at the trade deadline, partaking in a three-team blockbuster that sent budding shortstop Jose Iglesias to the Tigers and brought White Sox veteran righty **Jake Peavy** to Boston in return.

Trading for the former Cy Young winner paid dividends immediately as Peavy went 3-1 with a 3.18 ERA in his first month in a Red Sox uniform. His capstone performance came on Aug. 25 at Dodger Stadium, where he shut down a fearsome Los Angeles lineup with a complete-game, three-hit, five-strikeout effort en route to an 8-1 Red Sox win.

Also making his Red Sox debut in August was highly touted infield prospect Xander Bogaerts. At just 20 years old, the Aruba native began the season with Double-A Portland (Maine), hitting .311 with a .407 OBP, good enough for a June call-up to Triple-A Pawtucket (R.I.), where he hit .284 in 60 contests. In his first 50 Major League plate appearances, Bogaerts hit a respectable .250 with a homer and five RBI, spelling a bright future on the left side of the Red Sox infield.

In the present, the hottest Red Sox bat in August belonged to 30-year-old Daniel Nava. The outfielder began the month with a walk-off single on the first day — capping a six-run, ninth-inning rally — and ended it having batted .396 with a .473 OBP, leading the team in both categories.

SEPTEMBER 2013

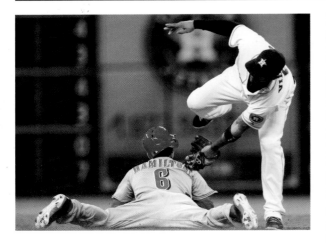

FAST START

Cincinnati call-up **Billy Hamilton** went 3 for 4 and stole four bases in his first career start on Sept. 18, becoming the first player since 1920 to accomplish the latter. He finished the regular season with 13.

WILD FINISH

On Sept. 29, Miami pitcher Henderson Alvarez sealed the club's fifth no-no — but not from the mound. Although he held Detroit hitless through nine, the game remained scoreless until Greg Dobbs, pinch-hitting with the bases loaded and two outs, watched a wild pitch go by for the sixth walk-off no-no since 1901.

LATE SHOW

Matt Adams hit home runs in the 14th and 16th innings of a 5-4 Cardinals win on Sept. 4 to become the first player in franchise history to hit two extra-inning longballs in one game. The feat also made him the first in MLB history to hit two homers after the 14th inning in the same game.

PERFECT ENDINGS

Boston's **Koji Uehara** struck out Robinson Cano on Sept. 6 to record his 27th straight out dating back to Aug. 17 — a closer's equivalent of a perfect game.

IT ALMOST FELT like the Red Sox were being spoiled when — with the club already well on its way to a bounce-back season the likes of which few teams had ever accomplished — **Clay Buchholz** returned after spending more than two months on the DL.

Buchholz was 9-0 with a 1.71 ERA in 12 starts before going down in June with a neck injury, and did not skip a beat upon his return, arming the Red Sox with yet another tool in their loaded shed. In four September starts, he went 3-1 with a 1.88 ERA, finishing the season a sterling 12-1 with a 1.74 ERA and 1.03 WHIP in 108.1 innings pitched.

But the most impressive late-season pitching performance came from the bullpen, where Koji Uehara — who began the season third on the closer depth chart behind Joel Hanrahan and Andrew Bailey — pieced together one of the finest pitching stretches ever. From July 9 to Sept. 13, Uehara tossed 30.1 consecutive scoreless innings, converting all 14 of his save opportunities over that span.

And that was just the second most impressive streak Uehara strung together late in the season, as he retired 37 batters in a row from Aug. 17 through Sept. 13, which would be a starter's equivalent of a perfect game, plus 10 more batters. He finished the season with a Major League–record 0.57 WHIP (min. 50 IP), proving himself as one of the most essential cogs in Boston's new well-oiled machine.

That machine constructed a dream season, as the Red Sox finished 97-65, 28 wins better than 2012 and tops in the Major Leagues.

WILD CARDS

NATIONAL LEAGUE, OCT. 1
PIRATES 6, REDS 2

THE PITTSBURGH FAITHFUL MADE SURE THEY WERE heard at PNC Park for the first Pirates playoff game since 1992, as their thunderous chants of "Cueee-tooo," visibly rattled Reds starter Johnny Cueto in the second inning.

In his first-ever playoff at-bat, 12-year veteran Marlon Byrd took Cueto deep to put Pittsburgh on the board. Two batters later, with Russell Martin at the plate, Cueto dropped the ball as he tried to come set, sending the fans into an uproar. Martin crushed the next pitch into left field, and suddenly the Pirates had an early 2-0 lead with 16-game winner Francisco Liriano on the hill.

Liriano struck out five over seven innings, allowing just one run on an RBI single by Jay Bruce that scored Shin-Soo Choo. Choo added a homer in the eighth off reliever Tony Watson, but shutdown closer Jason Grilli came on in the ninth and set the Reds down in order to secure the win and a trip to the NLDS.

	1	2	3	4	5	6	7	8	9	R	H	E
CINCINNATI	0	0	0	1	0	0	0	1	0	2	6	0
PITTSBURGH	0	2	1	2	0	0	1	0	x	6	14	0

WP: Liriano LP: Cueto
HR: CIN: Choo; PIT: Byrd, Martin (2)

Fernando Rodney

AMERICAN LEAGUE, OCT. 2
RAYS 4, INDIANS 0

AFTER WINNING A TIE-BREAKER GAME AGAINST TEXAS behind a complete-game gem from David Price, the Rays sent young Alex Cobb to the mound hoping he would pull off something similar. Less than four months after taking a line drive to the head, which sidelined him for two months, Cobb delivered, dominating the Indians over 6.2 shutout innings. The big blow came from Rays outfielder Desmond Jennings, who hit a two-run double off Indians starter Danny Salazar in the fourth inning.

Salazar came out of the gate firing for Cleveland as he set down the first six Rays hitters in order, three on punchouts. The Indians made some noise in the bottom of the seventh with back-to-back singles by Yan Gomes and Lonnie Chisenhall, but failed to capitalize. Cobb and the Rays' bullpen shut out the Cleveland offense, despite the Indians out-hitting the Rays, 9-8. A date with the Boston Red Sox in the ALDS awaited Tampa.

	1	2	3	4	5	6	7	8	9	R	H	E
TAMPA BAY	0	0	1	2	0	0	0	0	1	4	8	0
CLEVELAND	0	0	0	0	0	0	0	0	0	0	9	1

WP: Cobb LP: Salazar
HR: TB: Young

B STRONG

In the wake of an early-season tragedy, the Red Sox became a unifying force for the city of Boston.

THE "BOSTON STRONG" LOGO ON FENWAY PARK'S Green Monster, added in the wake of the Boston Marathon bombings, symbolizes the city's resilience in a time of tragedy. Since the April 15, 2013, attack, MLB and the Boston Red Sox used their resources to help those affected.

On the day after the bombing, the Sox took on the Indians at Progressive Field and hung a Boston Strong jersey bearing the city's 617 area code in the visiting dugout. Throughout the season, victims and first responders were invited to Fenway Park to partake in pregame activities and throw out ceremonial first pitches. According to Dr. Charles Steinberg, the Red Sox's executive vice president and a senior advisor to the President/CEO, the team was involved in 470 community appearances this season, including hospital visits to victims.

Major League Baseball pledged $500,000 to The One Fund Boston, a relief organization established in the aftermath of the tragedy. MLB licensee Brand 47 produced hats featuring the B Strong logo, donating 100 percent of the proceeds to the fund. The Red Sox also got involved, making a $100,000 contribution.

As longtime Red Sox star David Ortiz petitioned in not-so-subtle language to a packed Fenway crowd when the club returned home from its three-game set in Cleveland, "This is our [expletive] city! Stay strong."

Ortiz (above) and the rest of the Red Sox found renewed pride in their city in the wake of the Boston Marathon tragedy.

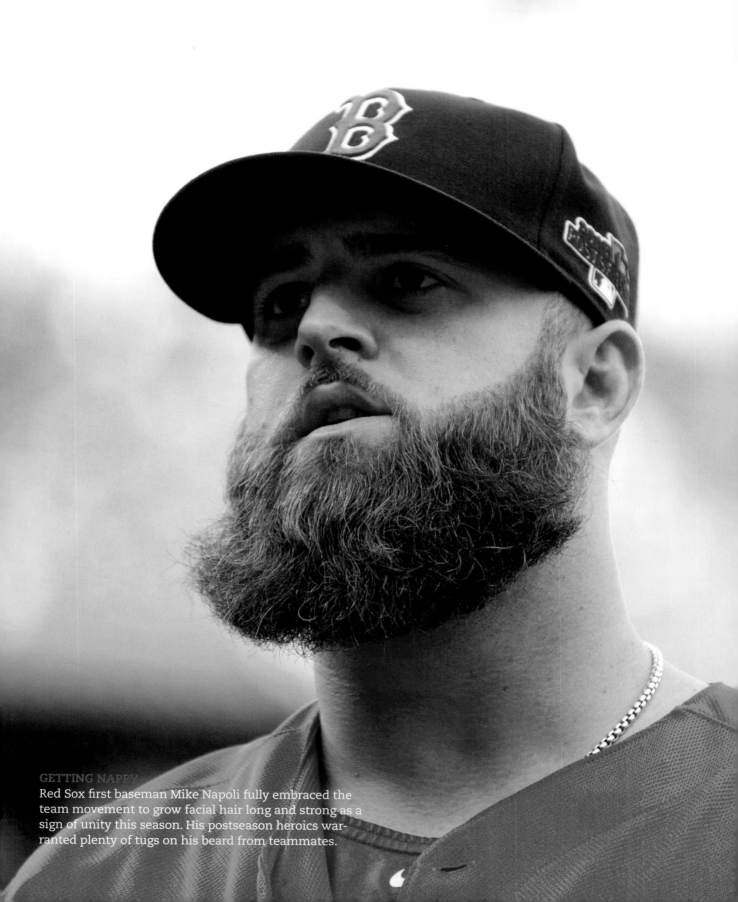

Red Sox first baseman Mike Napoli fully embraced the
team movement to grow facial hair long and strong as a
sign of unity this season. His postseason heroics war-
ranted plenty of tugs on his beard from teammates.

MANE ATTRACTIONS

A wild array of beards put a quirky new face on the game this season, and the Sox were the hairiest of the bunch.

IF BALLPLAYERS WERE REGARDED AS HARBINGERS of the latest fashion trends, it would be obvious that a bearded profile was *the look* of 2013. From the well coiffed, neatly trimmed type favored by David Ortiz, to the shaggy caveman style embraced by Mike Napoli, players around the Majors — and the Red Sox in particular — have been fully on board with the facial hair resurgence. It may not be the Yankees' look of choice — third baseman Kevin Youkilis, a Boston transplant, had to shave his signature goatee when he joined the Bronx Bombers this past off-season — but it certainly has caught on elsewhere. Even seemingly clean-cut Phillies pitcher Cole Hamels donned a thick 1970s-style mustache during Spring Training. (The American Mustache Institute calls it the "chevron.") Whether the style serves to perpetuate unshaven indifference or maintain a well crafted image varies — Josh Collmenter's beard fit right in at the Arizona Renaissance Festival — either type appears here to stay.

STRENGTH IN LOCKS

"I have two jobs," A's right fielder Josh Reddick wrote in his Twitter bio early this season. "Play baseball and BEAT [professional wrestler] DANIEL BRYAN IN A BEARDOFF!" The contest was short-lived, as Reddick trimmed the beard in late April, but the locks were auctioned to benefit autism awareness.

MANE ATTRACTIONS

HAIR-RAISING
Clockwise from top left: Once adorned by a crown of dreadlocks, Jose Reyes got a fresh cut when he joined the Marlins in 2012. With Toronto, he was back to letting his hair down — although this time, it grew off his chin. Beards abounded in the AL East this season, as Red Sox teammates Jonny Gomes and David Ortiz were just two of the club's folically blessed players. Gomes' choice aligned with Boston's fear-the-shears mentality, while Ortiz's signature chinstrap made it into *Sports Illustrated*'s Facial Hair Hall of Fame. The Nationals' Jayson Werth had quite an accomplished mane of his own, earning him the nickname "Werewolf."

> "GUYS WITH BEARDS ARE PRETTY TOUGH IN GENERAL. I THINK IT'S AN HONOR FOR SOMEONE TO GRAB YOUR BEARD WITH THEIR HANDS FULL OF PINE TAR."
>
> Jonny Gomes

HARP'S HAIR

For young Nationals outfielder Bryce Harper, it's all about the game face. Frequently donning slick eye-black and a fierce stare, his intensity is always on display. And the whole package comes together with his hair. What started out as a mohawk and soul patch transformed into a full beard with a combination faux-hawk/pompadour, which Harper sported after tweeting, "I need a Rockabilly barbershop in DC! Anybody? #haircut." Like teammate Werth, Harper's hair has inspired its own Twitter account.

THE TOAST OF BEANTOWN

From triumphs to struggles and back again, Dustin Pedroia has endured it all during his tenure in Boston. This year's return to glory and a new contract extension promise to keep the bond between the city and its second baseman tight.

RED SOX SECOND BASEMAN DUSTIN PEDROIA TASTED success from almost the instant he got to the Major Leagues. The Woodland, Calif. native reeled in a Rookie of the Year Award and a World Series trophy in 2007. The next year, he won the American League MVP Award, as the Red Sox came within a game of getting back to the Fall Classic. After a third straight postseason appearance in 2009, it seemed that the good times would never stop rolling.

But while Pedroia maintained his individual success over the years, Boston as a team hit some bumps from 2010–12. That's what has made the 2013 season such a special one for the Red Sox and their fiery second baseman. During a recent sit-down with Major League Baseball, Pedroia reflected on the memories of his first World Series and his coming of age in one of America's most baseball-rich cities.

After so much early success in your career, how hard was it for both you and the team to miss the postseason three years in a row?
The first two years we didn't make the playoffs seemed like torture. We had a bunch of injuries in 2010, and in 2011, we were one game away. Our main focus this year was just to win as many games as possible, and we were good about keeping that same mindset each day throughout the season.

Did the team's struggles the last few years make you appreciate this year more?
Yeah. It stinks at the time you're going through it, but you learn a lot. You learn what to stay away from.

What was it like to play in the World Series as a rookie?
It happened so fast. Those four days felt like they were all wrapped into one. I think it's because in the Cleveland series (ALCS) we were down, 3-1, and it seemed like we were a minute from being out of it. Then, all of a sudden, we just kept playing. That was our main focus: make sure we get to play the next day. Sure enough, we won the World Series, and it still felt like we had more games to play. It was a blast.

How about hitting a leadoff home run in your first World Series at-bat?
That was crazy. It was the first inning and I was just trying to get on base. It was really cold. I hit it well, but I didn't think I hit it well enough to get out; I thought it was going to hit the top of the wall and be a double. It just barely got out. It was pretty cool.

You were part of the organization in 2004. Do you remember watching that historic run on TV?
Yeah, I watched it all. You always pull for the team that drafts you.

"THE TEAMS THAT ARE IN IT YEAR IN AND YEAR OUT AND GO DEEP IN THE PLAYOFFS ARE RELENTLESS IN THEIR APPROACH."

I remember thinking that if they could just win Game 4 of the ALCS, their pitching was lined up with shutdown guys the next two games. And in Game 7, one game, anything can happen. They came out and jumped on [the Yankees] and swung the bats great. I was rooting hard for the Red Sox.

The "Laser Show" nickname has taken on a life of its own. You seem to embrace it judging by your Twitter handle (@15Lasershow). Tell us how that got started.
We would say stuff like that in college, when you're using those aluminum bats. Those are like weapons. Sometimes I'd joke around about it in front of the media if we were just hanging out in the dugout.

But the first time I really said it publicly, in front of all the microphones and cameras, was in 2010 when David Ortiz was in a slump and I was sticking up for him. I reminded everyone that in my rookie year I didn't hit at all the first month of the season. And then I added, "What happened after that? Laser Show." It was pretty funny the way it stuck.

What's the biggest difference between the style of play in the regular season and the playoffs?
Everything is a little bit faster. Pitchers don't hold back. They're going to give all their velocity. They're going to be careful of where to throw the ball. Scouting reports are more magnified. It's the same thing with offensive approach. We're always prepared, but we'll be more prepared on each pitcher, what he tries to do and what his tendencies are. It's a big game within the game — that makes it fun.

Is there a common thread between championship teams?
They're all relentless. Whether offensively, defensively or through their pitching, the teams that are in it year in and year out and go deep in the playoffs are relentless in what they do and they believe in their approach.

People call you Boston's Derek Jeter in terms of what you mean to your team. How do you feel about that comparison?
If you ask every single player, he's the guy they admire the most. He goes out there and plays the game the right way. He treats everyone with respect and plays hard. I know he's with the Yankees and our fans hate the Yankees, but we all love him. He's done so much for baseball and everybody appreciates that. [Being compared to Jeter is] probably the biggest compliment you can have.

How much do you enjoy watching the influx of young stars like Mike Trout, Manny Machado and Bryce Harper?
It's awesome. We played against Trout a few times and saw Machado a lot. We played against Harper in 2012. Their talent level is through the roof. Those guys are going to carry the game for 20 years. It's pretty cool to watch them. I remember watching Ken Griffey Jr. as a kid. With guys like that, it seems like they're playing Little League. They bring that stuff every night.

You recently signed a contract that should keep you with the Red Sox through 2021. How much peace of mind does that give you?
It's great. It's nice to know I'm going to be here, hopefully for my whole career. I always wanted to be. But I don't look into it too much. I'm always working so that I don't ever take a step back.

You and David Ortiz must have a pretty strong relationship. What has it been like going through the ups and downs with him over the years?
It's been awesome. I've hit in front of him for most of my career so far, except for the first year when I hit leadoff. He cares about winning and that bonds us together.

At the same time, he has fun and makes you take a step back and try to realize that the game is fun and you should enjoy playing it. When you're struggling, he pulls

Pedroia has brought two World Series championships to Fenway Park in his seven seasons with the Red Sox.

you out of it. He's always there for you as a teammate and a friend. It's a pretty special relationship.

How did the Boston Marathon tragedy in April affect team chemistry and clubhouse atmosphere?
After that, we felt like we were playing for a lot more. You always have responsibility when you play for the Red Sox, but it just felt like more even when we went into funks. On a road trip in August, we went to San Francisco and they had an emotional ceremony on the field recognizing what happened in Boston. That reminds you what you're playing for and what the city went through earlier in the year. You don't want to let anyone down.

You've been close friends with Dodgers outfielder Andre Ethier since college. Tell us about that.
In the offseason, we work out and hit together just about every day. We live close to each other, so our kids often spend time together. During the season, we talk probably two or three times a month. If either of us is struggling, we'll shoot each other a text: "What do you see?" — things like that.

It's crazy that 10 years ago we were playing in college together, and this year we were both on playoff teams in the Big Leagues. We pull for each other. Sometimes I'll go home and watch his games after ours because of the time difference.

After turning 30 this year, do you feel like you're in more of a position to be a mentor?
If I need to say something, I'll say it. For the most part, you have to go out there and play the game right and guys will hopefully follow. That's the only thing I'm thinking about.

Who did you learn from coming up?
We had a bunch of guys — Mike Lowell, Jason Varitek, Alex Cora — who helped me a ton along the way.

As much as you've accomplished already, in what ways are you still looking to improve?
Just my consistency. Year in and year out, if I go out and do what I'm supposed to do, I'll be where I want to be. I want to make sure I'm like that every single season and I work hard to try to accomplish that.

MINOR LEAGUE RESULTS

AAA PAWTUCKET RED SOX (80-63)

1st in International League North Division

AA PORTLAND SEA DOGS (68-73)

4th in Eastern League Eastern Division

HIGH-A SALEM RED SOX (76-64)

2nd in Carolina League Southern Division
Swept Potomac Nationals to win the championship

CLASS-A GREENVILLE DRIVE (51-87)

7th in South Atlantic League Southern Division

CLASS-A SHORT SEASON LOWELL SPINNERS (40-33)

2nd in New York–Penn League Stedler Division

MAJOR LEAGUE BASEBALL PROPERTIES

Senior Vice President, Consumer Products	**HOWARD SMITH**
Vice President, Publishing	**DONALD S. HINTZE**
Editorial Director	**MIKE McCORMICK**
Publications Art Director	**FAITH M. RITTENBERG**
Senior Production Manager	**CLAIRE WALSH**
Account Executive, Publishing	**CHRIS RODDAY**
Senior Publishing Coordinator	**JAKE SCHWARTZSTEIN**
Associate Art Director	**MARK CALIMBAS**
Associate Editor	**ALLISON DUFFY**
Project Assistant Editors	**BRIAN KOTLOFF**
	JORDAN RABINOWITZ
Project Designer	**JENIFER COZZOLINO**
Editorial Intern	**ANTHONY RUGGIERO**

MAJOR LEAGUE BASEBALL PHOTOS

Manager	**JESSICA FOSTER**
Photo Editor	**JIM McKENNA**
Intern	**JARED SILBER**

THE FENN / McCLELLAND & STEWART TEAM

Publisher, FENN	**C. JORDAN FENN**
President & CEO	**BRAD MARTIN**
EVP, Executive Publisher, M&S Doubleday Canada Publishing Group	**KRISTIN COCHRANE**
Executive Managing Editor	**ELIZABETH KRIBS**
VP, Director of Production	**JANINE LAPORTE**
Senior Production Coordinator	**VALENTINA CAPUANI**
EVP, Director of Sales	**DUNCAN SHIELDS**
Director of Sales	**JAMES YOUNG**
Publicity Manager	**RUTA LIORMONAS**
Director, Online Marketing	**CASSANDRA SADEK**
Director, Special Promotions and Marketing	**RANDY CHAN**
Publicity Manager, Marketing Lead	**ASHLEY DUNN**

**WORLD SERIES
CONTRIBUTING PHOTOGRAPHERS**

David Durochik

Brad Mangin

Rob Tringali

Ron Vesely
